HORIZON

SEPTEMBER, 1962 · VOLUME V, NUMBER 1

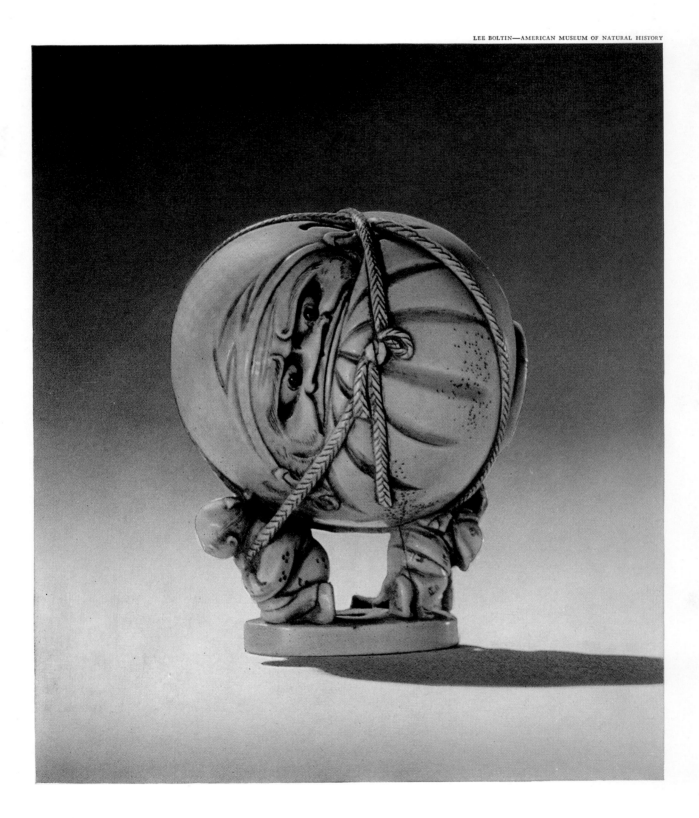

HORIZON

A Magazine of the Arts

SEPTEMBER, 1962 · VOLUME V, NUMBER 1

PUBLISHER
James Parton

EDITORIAL DIRECTOR
Joseph J. Thorndike, Jr.

EDITOR
William Harlan Hale

MANAGING EDITOR
Eric Larrabee

ASSOCIATE EDITOR
Ralph Backlund

ASSISTANT EDITORS
Ada Pesin
Jane Wilson
Albert Bermel

CONTRIBUTING EDITOR
Margery Darrell

EDITORIAL ASSISTANTS
Shirley Abbott, Caroline Backlund
Wendy Buehr, Charles L. Mee, Jr.

COPY EDITOR
Mary Ann Pfeiffer
Assistants: Joan Rehe, Ruth H. Wolfe

ART DIRECTOR
Irwin Glusker
Associate Art Director: Elton Robinson

ADVISORY BOARD
Gilbert Highet, *Chairman*
Frederick Burkhardt   Oliver Jensen
Marshall B. Davidson   Jotham Johnson
Richard M. Ketchum   John Walker

EUROPEAN CONSULTING EDITOR
J. H. Plumb
Christ's College, Cambridge

EUROPEAN BUREAU
Gertrudis Feliu, *Chief*
11 rue du Bouloi, Paris

HORIZON is published every two months by American
Heritage Publishing Co., Inc. Executive and editorial
offices: 551 Fifth Ave., New York 17, N.Y. HORIZON
welcomes contributions but can assume no responsibility for unsolicited material.

All correspondence about subscriptions should be
addressed to: HORIZON Subscription Office, 379 West
Center St., Marion, Ohio.

Single Copies: $4.50
Annual Subscriptions: $21.00 in the U.S. & Can.
$22.00 elsewhere

An annual index is published every September, priced
at $1. HORIZON is also indexed in the *Readers Guide
to Periodical Literature.*

Title registered U.S. Patent Office

Second-class postage paid at New York, N.Y., and
at additional mailing offices.

MAN'S FIRST REVOLUTION	*John Pfeiffer*	4
MAN'S FIRST MURALS	*James Mellaart*	10
THE NON-TEACHERS	*Robert Bendiner*	14
A MEMORANDUM: FROM EMPRESS EUGENIE TO JACQUELINE KENNEDY	*William Harlan Hale*	20
THROUGH THE GLASS BRIGHTLY	*Wolf Von Eckardt*	22
MAKING A CULT OF CONFUSION	*Walter Kerr*	33
WHERE WILL THE BOOKS GO?	*John Rader Platt*	42
CHINA OF THE CHINESE	*Brian Brake*	48
ARCHITECT'S HERO: LOUIS KAHN	*Albert Bush-Brown*	57
IN PRINT: EDWARD ADLER	*Gilbert Millstein*	64
ON STAGE: JOAN BAEZ	*Judith Milan*	66
THE MAN WHO CLEANED UP SHAKESPEARE	*E. M. Halliday*	68
WHEN ISLAM RULED IBERIA	*Gerald Brenan*	72
CHILD OF THE FAR FRONTIER	*Wallace Stegner*	94
ARTIST FROM THE OUTBACK	*Alan Moorehead*	96
AN INVITATION: BURGESS HILL SCHOOL		105
MOVIES: THE ART OF GOING IT ALONE	*Saul Bellow*	108
THEATRE: ON BEING UPSTAGED BY SCENERY	*Robert Hatch*	110
BOOKS: HISTORY BY ANOTHER NAME	*Gilbert Highet*	112
CHANNELS: TWO CHEERS FOR MEDIOCRITY	*Stephen White*	114
COME OVER AND SEE FOR YOURSELF	*Drawings by William Charmatz*	116
ENCODE ME, MY SWEET ENCODABLE YOU	*William K. Zinsser*	120

COVER: This preliminary sketch by Marc Chagall, in vivid pictorial shorthand, shows one of the twelve stained-glass windows with which he created a crown of light for a new synagogue in Jerusalem. Chagall's windows are a high-water mark of the current revival in the art of stained glass, which is described in an article beginning on page 22.

FRONTISPIECE: The face in the ropes is that of Bodhidharma, or Daruma, the Buddhist mystic who founded the sect of Zen in China in the fifth century. While Zen was later adopted in Japan, folk tales there made Daruma an object of ridicule, as is often the fate of professional wise men. Daruma had been revered for a feat of meditation lasting nine years, but the Japanese said that nothing was left of him afterward but his head, which his disciples were obliged to carry about on their backs. The story persisted in folk art. This Japanese version, two inches high, dates from the early nineteenth century. It is a *netsuke*, an ivory piece designed to be fastened to the strings of a purse or tobacco pouch.

It was agricultural, and it changed him from a primitive hunter into a communal being with time and impulse for art. Recent Near Eastern finds, dating back ten millennia, are rapidly revising our ideas about the dawn of civilization

MAN'S

Some of the first farmers and villagers lived about 9,000 years ago in and about the Zagros Mountains, on the border between present-day Iran and Iraq. Such communities as Tepe Sarab, shown above in the process of being excavated, have furnished new knowledge of how important agriculture was as the road to early culture. Opposite, left, a clay imprint from Jarmo, Iraq (c. 7000–6500 B.C.) provides the first evidence of domesticated wheat in that germinal region of man's advance. The plant is structurally similar to the wild wheat (opposite, right) that grows there today.

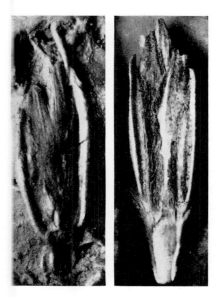

OPPOSITE: ROBERT J. BRAIDWOOD; ABOVE: HANS HELBAEK, DANISH NATIONAL MUSEUM

By JOHN PFEIFFER

FIRST REVOLUTION

The first fundamental change in human economy—the revolution that changed man from a primitive, hand-to-mouth food gatherer to a community-dwelling individual on his way to "civilization"—seems to have occurred about nine thousand years ago. As long as man ate only what he could kill or pick in the wilds, he depended on the precarious balance of nature; his numbers were limited by the numbers of other living things. He flourished when nature was bountiful and declined in times of local scarcity. For all his wits and skills, he shared with lesser animals an utter dependence on factors beyond his control. Getting food was often a full-time, unremitting occupation, with energies focused intensively on the life-or-death business of wringing the last bit of nourishment from the earth. However, as soon as he learned to grow his own crops and raise his own livestock, he began to control his universe. He was blessed with free time, time to devise new implements and crafts, to concentrate on hitherto elusive ideas, to shape new ways of life.

This change, the beginning of agriculture, accelerated the pace of man's evolution: communities of farmers and herdsmen were rapidly replacing scavenging nomads by 5000 B.C., and in the next millennium or two irrigation came to the valleys, rapidly followed by crop rotation, the use of fertilizers, beer and bread, dairy products—and writing, cities, temples, and dynasties. The rise of man may be compared to the flight of a rocket that lifts slowly and almost reluctantly from its launching place, picks up momentum, and then soars with a rush into space. Man's slow rise, from early half-apes to the appearance of *Homo sapiens,* took more than a million years. The soaring started with the agricultural revolution.

The first farmers, inevitably, left scant evidence of their way of life. They lived simply, and most of the things they left behind are inconspicuous. There are no royal tombs or temples, inscriptions to decipher, masks and goblets of gold, precious jewels. Indeed, it is a formidable task simply to locate their settlements and, having located them, to know what sort of evidence to look for. But in the past few years teams of geologists, botanists, zoologists, and archaeologists have been piecing together scraps and clues that point toward new ideas and prickly new questions concerning this crucial phase of man's development. The center of activity lies in the foothills and gulches of the Zagros Mountains, on the border between Iraq and Iran. Working in and around this area, Robert J. Braidwood, of the University of Chicago's Oriental Institute, and a team of specialists have found two hundred fifty prehistoric sites. Newspaper headlines have described recent discoveries by James Mellaart, who is affiliated with the Ankara Archaeological Museum in Turkey, Jean Perrot of the French Archaeological Mission in Israel, and Ralph Solecki of Columbia University.

Archaeologists are finding religious objects, rare frescoes, hunting equipment and household wares, microlithic flint blades, beads, bracelets, rings, and bone needles. There are grass-cutting blades, mortars and pestles, milling stones, and circular stone houses. There is, in these discoveries, evidence of man's settling in villages, domesticating animals, and beginning to form self-sustaining agricultural communities. There is evidence of the way he lived, evolved, and laid the foundations of Western civilization in the valleys of the Nile, the Tigris, and the Euphrates.

Agriculture enabled man to break loose from his environment, to create new kinds of abundance. Since food plants and animals in the wild must compete with other species, their numbers are limited accordingly. But once domestication or farming eliminated the competition, they were free to multiply enormously. A steady and dynamic increase replaced the sporadic abundance of nature, and man multiplied in proportion to his food supplies. There were "surplus" people, more than enough to run the farms, to grind cereals, to build houses, to think, to make sculpture, to paint (see "Man's First Murals" by James Mellaart, on page 10), and—eventually—to write.

The leaders of the agricultural revolution and their ancestors were to be found, nine to ten thousand years ago, in various parts of the world. In Middle America they were just beginning to cultivate maize, beans, and squashes. The domestication of taro, yams, breadfruit, and possibly rice took place at about the same time in southeastern Asia, perhaps in Malaya or Burma. But the Near East has a special significance. For one thing, it was here that the change appeared first. For another, we are what we are largely because of developments that took place in this part of the world and then spread to Europe. The crucial, or nuclear, Near Eastern area included a two-thousand-mile arc sweeping northwest from near the Persian Gulf along the Zagros Mountains, across southern Turkey, and down the east coast of the Mediterranean through Syria, Lebanon, and Israel. An extension, or wing, of the arc stretched five hundred miles due west along the southern coast of Turkey.

Generally speaking, the critical part of the agricultural revolution seems to have occurred in three stages:

(1) The end of food-collecting: a stage of increasing ingenuity in living on wild plants and animals. 15000 B.C. to 9000 B.C.

(2) Incipient cultivation and domestication: the beginnings of food production, attempts to obtain new food sources by isolating and caring for selected plants and animals. 9000 B.C. to 7000 B.C.

(3) Primary village-farming communities: the establishment of the earliest permanent settlements in which domesticated plants and animals provided a significant part of the food supply. 7000 B.C. to 5000 B.C.

Since these stages merge with one another by as yet ill-defined steps, the dates are rough estimates only. But the broad picture appears to be valid and provides a framework for continuing research.

Braidwood and his associates have reconstructed the main outlines of this story as it occurred in the region near Kirkuk, Iraq, in the Zagros foothills about one hundred fifty miles north of Baghdad. For a period of several thousand years the snow line rose more than a mile as icecaps melted and exposed tiers of foothills, higher and higher ridges running parallel to one another like the ripples in a washboard. Trees and grasses crept up the ridges and into valleys set among the foothills, taking root in glacial deposits and spreading to altitudes of 2,000 to 5,000 feet. Among the animals to follow the plants was man, who reoccupied caves and rock shelters abandoned thousands of years earlier by his cave-man ancestors.

These people were forced to devote nearly all their energies to gleaning some food from the environment, and this necessity fostered numerous experiments in food-getting techniques. One sign of this development was a sharp rise in the number of so-called "microliths," carefully worked pygmy flints appearing at many sites. Only about half an inch to an inch long, they are too small to have been used singly and must have been set into shafts and handles to yield a wide variety of spiked and barbed cutting implements. Such elements indicate increasing sophistication in the design of tools and weapons, and hint at the beginning of the quest—culminating in domestication—for new food sources. As far as we know, domestication and cultivation were not yet being practiced twelve thousand years or so ago. The new techniques could not have been far off, however, especially considering the increased skill in exploiting food sources.

Many archaeologists suspect that plants were domesticated before animals. The argument is that farming requires a permanent or semipermanent home base, and that taking care of plants at even the most primitive level tends to bind people to a piece of land in a way that flocks and herds never could. It also creates some excess food for storage and at least the possibility of accumulating straw and fodder that might ultimately serve to nourish animals.

At the same time these people probably discovered that wheat and barley seeds gathered before the plants ripened fully are soft and milky and can be chewed "raw." Subsequent steps may have involved grinding ripened grains and storing supplies of seeds for the winter in corners of rock shelters. Now imagine that some of the stored seeds happened to take root in the disturbed earth of the shelters, say, in dump piles. When spring arrived, plants may have been seen growing in places where they had not grown be-

We are what we are, says the author of this article, largely because of early developments that took place in the Near East and then spread to Europe. Principal ancient sites mentioned in his text (and in "Man's First Murals" by James Mellaart, which follows on page 10) are located on the map opposite. Insert illustrations suggest the range of finds made at recently excavated sites—such as the dancer (c. 6000 B.C.) from the murals at Çatal Hüyük in Turkey, the fragmentary male figure from nearby Hacilar, a carved portrait-skull from Jericho, a clay pig from Tepe Sarab, and an agricultural sickle blade (7000–6500 E.C.) from Jarmo, Iraq.

fore. Assuming such observations on the part of people whose lives were concentrated on getting food, it may not have been long before someone thought of putting more seeds in the "magic spots" and later enlarging the spots.

As far as the domestication of animals is concerned, the original motive was probably something besides achieving a dependable supply of meat and hides. One theory holds that it all started with a natural desire to keep pets. Perhaps hunters brought wild kids or lambs back for the children to play with, as they still do today. That would have complicated life somewhat, because pets must be cared for and prevented from feeding on cultivated plants. Young animals would thus represent a new responsibility.

Then people might have been confronted with an unpleasant but necessary decision. If food became scarce or animals became too difficult to handle as they grew older, the pets would have to be killed. Experiences of this sort could gradually lead to the idea of breeding animals with the specific purpose of using them for food. This theory applies to species like sheep and goats, which probably had no obvious practical value to families in the beginning—and which may have been the first domesticated animals.

But the odds are that other species were domesticated for other reasons. It is possible that hunters, feeling the need for an aid in tracking game, deliberately tamed certain species of wolves and created the dog as a kind of living artifact. The ancestors of ducks, geese, and other fowl may have been used primarily as decoys. After the establishment of herds and flocks, it would be a natural process to decide against unmanageable and aggressive animals in favor of those that happened to be easy to control.

Evidence to prove or disprove these and other plausible guesses is difficult to come by, and even more difficult to interpret. For example, a decade or so ago an expedition under Braidwood's direction located an important open-air site, not far from Kirkuk, known as Karim Shahir. About thirty thousand artifacts were found there, including many microlithic flint blades and flakes as well as beads, bracelets, pendants, rings, and some needles made of bone.

Together with these objects are also traces of something new, the transition from food-collecting to food-producing. A few of the blades have a characteristic luster, or "sickle sheen," on their sharp edges that can be produced only by cutting the stalks of cereal grasses; and there are crude hoelike implements known as celts, and fragments of mortars and pestles and milling stones. While these artifacts may have been used to cut and prepare wild cereals, they appear to indicate, because of the context in which they were found, the presence of domesticated plants.

At this stage of prehistory, around 9000 B.C., no simple story emerges. The archaeologist must work in terms of the entire constellation of things found, and the general feel he acquires for the site and its surroundings. The implements could have been used for far different purposes than we imagine. We get only a complex of subtle and sometimes conflicting clues. Some of the pebbles brought to the three-acre site from other places are arranged in "a sort of closely set pseudo-pavement," which implies that the inhabitants had settled down on at least a semipermanent basis. On the other hand the excavated layers seldom extended more than fourteen to fifteen inches beneath the surface, suggesting that the site may not have been occupied very long or else functioned as a seasonal camping place. Then there is another significant finding. The proportion of bones of animals that would become familiar on farms of the future is far higher here than at sites dating back to earlier times.

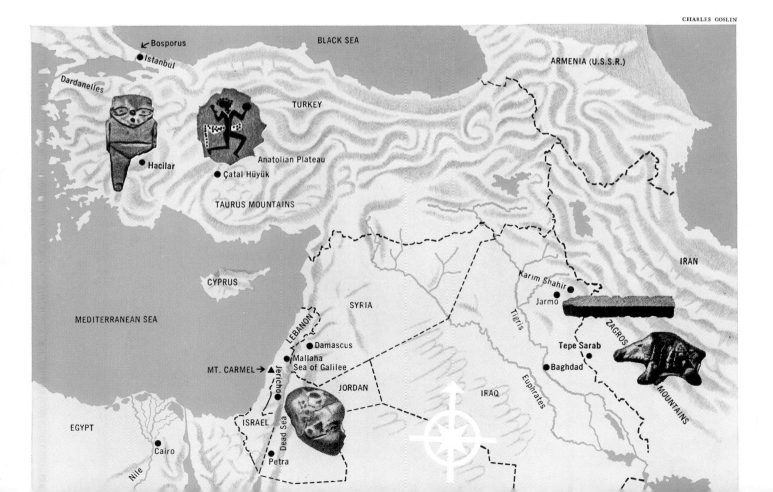

Sites in the same general region supplement the findings at Karim Shahir. The occupants of one site, excavated by Ralph Solecki of Columbia University, may have had domesticated sheep as early as 8900 B.C. Although these findings are still undergoing investigations that involve complex studies of the animals' foot bones, they will provide, if confirmed, the earliest direct evidence of domestication.

New sites currently being studied, and still described in preliminary reports only, are Beldibi near the southern coast of Turkey (the first excavation in that country representing early attempts at farming) and a site at Petra in southwest Jordan. The somewhat more recent site of Mallaha, located a few miles from Lake Galilee, is being excavated by Jean Perrot, who also directed work on later subterranean villages in the Negev (see HORIZON, January, 1962).

Throughout this period people lived more and more in the open. For a long time they had been coming out of caves and rock shelters when the weather was warm, although they were cautious enough as a rule to stay very near home base. On the terrace in front of one Mount Carmel shelter in Israel, for example, there are two curved rows of stones that might have served as benches or walls, and a stoned-off area for a hearth. But the tendency to break away completely seems to have become increasingly strong.

The changeover is represented by a whole range of building activities from the pseudo-pavements at Karim Shahir to far more advanced structures at Mallaha, which include well-cemented, circular stone houses more than twenty feet in diameter. New kinds of architecture accompany the slow development of permanent out-of-doors settlements and the beginnings of cultivation and domestication.

The next stage, the appearance of village-farming communities, is represented by fewer sites than the two preceding stages. Braidwood and his colleagues spent the better part of three seasons at Jarmo, one of the key Zagros foothill sites, and excavated more than a quarter of a million cubic yards of dirt. Although they stopped excavating the site about seven years ago, the artifacts found have provided material for continuing research ever since and even now have not been fully analyzed. Among the most important findings are numerous sickle blades, stone bowls, many varieties of milling stones, celts, and mortars and pestles—and the first direct signs of cultivated plants.

Ovens excavated at Jarmo may have been used, among other things, in preparing cereal grain for eating. The shucks of wild and early cultivated wheats fitted very tightly over the grains, and whole spikelets may have been tossed into an oven so that they could be popped like popcorn. Another type of artifact may also have been connected with farming: the site has yielded more than 5,000 fragments of figurines molded out of clay and representing animals and humans. According to one theory they may have been amulets intended to be buried in fields to help make things grow.

The Jarmo people lived in houses made of "tauf," a mud mix containing straw or grass to prevent cracking, and they had special rooms, or bins, for storage of grain. The floors consisted of packed-down silt bedded with reeds, and at least one house had a door into the oven room—indicated by a recessed jamb and a mortarlike stone serving as a socket in which the swivel post of the door could turn.

A number of similar sites have been discovered, one of them by a Danish expedition in the Jarmo region. In fact, Braidwood is convinced that the new technology based on cultivation and domestication was being developed in many such villages scattered over the nuclear areas of the Near East. Recently James Mellaart has done work at two Jarmo-like sites—Hacilar and Çatal Hüyük—located in the foothills of the Taurus Mountains, about fifty miles inland from Antalya on the southwest coast of Turkey.

The most impressive architectural findings come from one of the lowest levels of the Tell es-Sultan mound in the Dead Sea valley, the site of the Biblical city of Jericho. This level has been carbon dated at about 7000 B.C., which places it in the same period as Jarmo. Like the lower Jarmo layers, it contains sickle blades and other early equipment related to farming, but no pottery. But it is also distinguished by the sudden appearance of a fortified community rather than a little village, covering some eight acres and ringed by a stone wall five to six feet thick and about twice as high. There is also a great twenty-five-foot tower with an inner staircase leading to the top.

Such architecture could not have been achieved without a fairly advanced system of food production. Perrot and other archaeologists believe that Jericho is the result of an unusually fortunate combination of circumstances. The site is an oasis with an abundant water supply, located on an otherwise arid and desolate high terrace, and it may represent an

early farming and trading center for a widespread region.

One of the questions that arises is how domesticated species spread to outside areas, notably to Europe, where evolution had halted in its tracks. Here man was still in the food-collecting stage. He had attained his Golden Age some 20,000 years earlier in southwestern Europe, settling by the thousands along limestone cliffs, where he covered the walls of caves with magnificent paintings and engravings. But these people had vanished by the time of Jarmo. Their descendants roamed the same regions in small scattered bands, practiced a crude and unimpressive art—and perhaps, huddled at night around dying fires in little rock shelters, told legends of a glorious past. The decline was a result of climatic changes. Available food supplies dwindled, and so did the people and their works.

The people of Europe did not come into their own until agriculture spread in their direction from the Near East. Certainly trade and migration played a role in the process (for instance, across the Bosporus or Dardanelles, over the mountains of southeastern Yugoslavia, and down into the plains of the Danube). Yet the story has a great deal more to it. As a case in point, strains of cultivated wheat in the Near East were adapted to local climates, to wet winters and dry summers. European wheats were developed to be at home under radically different conditions—cold winters and perennially rainy and cold summers. In other words farmers along the way selected suitable variants and created new kinds of wheat. We know little about the bringing of wheat, barley, goats, and sheep to Europe; but it was probably under way by 6000 B.C. and took fifteen to twenty centuries.

Considerable research will be required to solve these and many other problems. The archaeologist is in the position of someone trying to deduce the plot of a motion picture, given only a few frames from the opening, middle, and closing sequences. There are series discontinuities, gaps in our knowledge. Most of the transitional steps from food-collecting to the beginnings of cultivation and domestication to village-farming communities, from Kirkuk to Karim Shahir to Jarmo, remain unknown; and new areas such as the region including the sources of the Tigris and Euphrates, which may represent another center of early agriculture, must be explored.

Special techniques will contribute more and more to future studies in the Near East, as well as in Middle America and elsewhere. Geologists are using pipelike equipment (originally developed for deep-sea explorations) to "punch out" cores of sediment twenty or more feet long from lake bottoms. The cores contain fossil pollens and microorganisms that flourished ten to twenty thousand years ago and may help to indicate local climatic changes in times past. Analyzing pottery fragments under the microscope may indicate whether clays came from local or outside sources and even reveal facts about agricultural practices, because straw and other plant materials were added to the clay to reduce stickiness and prevent cracking.

The story of civilization hinges upon painstaking attention to such details. This particular episode is perhaps the most important and exciting in the long course of human evolution. For implicit in the beginnings of agriculture is the genesis of Western civilization—the increasing time for man to spend in intellectual and artistic endeavors, the point of departure from primitivism toward a complex and sophisticated culture—in brief, the start of modern society.

John Pfeiffer, a free-lance science writer, is the author of Changing Universe *and* From Galaxies to Man.

When men acquired some leisure time, as a by-product of settled agriculture, they turned to making small statuettes. Their preoccupation with the still difficult task of getting food is reflected in much early art: both the fertility goddess, near left, and the clay sculpture representing a pig or boar, at far left, may have been designed to serve as good-luck charms or even idols to be worshiped. Both date from about 9,000 years ago. At right, a Near Eastern cylinder seal of a later period records the ritual of grain carrying, performed in the hope of increasing crop yields.

More than 8,000 years ago an artist painted on the wall of a village dwelling at Çatal Hüyük, in what is now Turkish Anatolia, a pioneer portrayal of the activities of his neolithic fellow men. The photograph below shows a detail of his work as recently discovered. At right is a sketched reconstruction of his mural as a whole: the inset square indicates the area of the original fragment below. The figures show men hunting, dancing, engaging in acrobatics, and beating a drum.

MAN'S FIRST MURALS

The scholar who recently discovered them presents startling works of
prehistoric art that were an indirect result of man's first revolution

Today we can no longer measure man's early cultural achievements only in terms of classical Greece or of the Bronze Age civilizations of Egypt, Mesopotamia, or Crete; new archaeological discoveries show that these eras had forerunners of no less importance. Among them is the highly sophisticated culture that flourished nine thousand years ago at Çatal Hüyük, a newly uncovered city on Turkey's Anatolian plateau. Dating from the Early Neolithic period, roughly 6600 to 5800 B.C., the Çatal Hüyük site has brought to light jewelry, hunting equipment, household utensils, statuettes and other religious objects, and—most significantly—the earliest murals ever found on man-made walls.

This center of art was found during an archaeological survey of the surrounding plain, which I led in 1958, and excavations there were begun in the summer of 1961. Although it will require another decade to uncover all of Çatal Hüyük, the largest neolithic site yet known in the Near East, the discoveries we have made thus far hint at the extraordinary achievement, at a very early date, that this site represents.

Çatal Hüyük covers thirty-two acres in the center of the fertile plain of Konya. Its people practiced agriculture, as well as stockbreeding, primarily of cattle. Their houses are crowded around courtyards or on narrow lanes, presenting a most urban appearance, and they are characterized by a convenience of layout that is strikingly "modern": two or more rooms, a raised platform, or divan, a bench, sometimes a plaster cupboard with shelves, a grain bin, and an isolated, meticulously arranged cooking area with a built-in wall oven. The growth of settled communities, brought about by the agricultural revolution (see the preceding article on this subject by John Pfeiffer), apparently provided an opportunity for the Çatal Hüyük dwellers to decorate their houses; and the ornamentation varies from panels, recesses, and painted hearths to, in one large building, work in plaster relief.

The character of this culture betrays a neatness, attention to detail, and sophistication far beyond what even the most sanguine of archaeologists would have expected to find at so early a period. And its wall paintings, illustrated on these pages, constitute its greatest surprise.

The paintings were executed on the interior walls of houses or shrines, with a brush, in freehand application of flat wash against white or cream-colored plaster, with a relatively wide assortment of colors that include shades of red, pink, mauve, white, buff, black, and—in one instance—pale yellow. Perhaps the most significant aspect of the art is that several different styles are evident, indicating the work of a number of different artists.

The earliest of the work now being recovered is purely geometric, similar to the designs on the woven mats or textiles also found at the site. In later works at Çatal Hüyük the human figure emerges: a group of four males dressed in white loincloths and animal skins, a small figure of a plump woman dressed in leopard skin, and some other fragments of figures and "portraits."

The more recent, and better preserved, paintings (shown opposite and on the two following pages) are almost exclusively concerned with hunting or hunting ritual scenes. One of the main panels in a shrinelike building contains a mural of considerable scope, depicting a number of men hunting red deer; a huge aurochs bull, six feet long, dominates one entire wall. But of all the paintings at Çatal Hüyük the mural on the east wall of this same shrine (opposite) must have been, at the time it was fully intact, the most spectacular. Even in the four slight fragments that survive there is evidence of outstanding technical dexterity. The earliest of the scenes shows thirteen men in three rows, performing a ritual dance in which they are disguised as leopards. The sense of motion in the dancing and acrobatics, and the rendering of true and distorted perspective in this and the deer-hunting scene (page 13), is remarkably well projected.

What is the origin of this art? Until investigations of Çatal Hüyük's earlier, lower levels are completed, it would be premature to offer even hypotheses. Nothing yet is known of the beginnings of the neolithic culture that flourished there only to become extinguished; nor do we know, from other excavations in Anatolia so far, whether the culture was any more than local.

Similarities have been pointed out between the Çatal Hüyük murals, the upper paleolithic Lascaux cave paintings in southern France (about 20,000 B.C.), and the neolithic Tassili frescoes in the Sahara (8000 to 3000 B.C.)*; and there is certainly an analogous preoccupation with lively scenes in which the human element is dominant. However, with so little knowledge of these early periods it may be unjustifiable to speculate about resemblances between expressions of art that are separated by such vast regions of what is still artistically, if not archaeologically, *terra incognita*.

With or without such formidable comparisons, Çatal Hüyük stands as an instance of man's emergence, in a very early community, through agriculture into art.

* See "Surprise in the Sahara," by Henri Lhote, in HORIZON for May, 1959.

11

By JAMES MELLAART

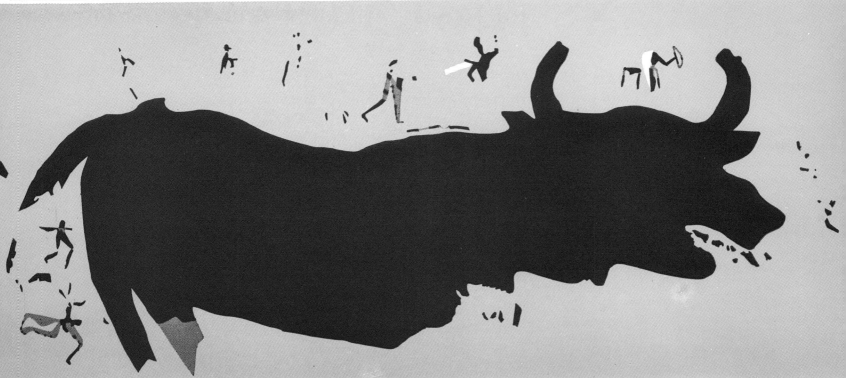

Though separated by thousands of years and thousands of miles from the new-found murals at Çatal Hüyük in Turkey, the cave painting of a bull at Lascaux in southern France (left) and the rendering of antelopes found at Tassili in North Africa (below) show a strong resemblance in style and spirit to such Çatal Hüyük figures as those shown here. Each culture apparently arrived at these similar themes and styles independently. The Lascaux cave painting dates from more than 20,000 years ago, the Tassili art from about 5,500 years ago, and the Çatal Hüyük murals from 8,000 to 9,000 years ago.

The enormous wall painting of an aurochs bull (opposite, in a sketched reconstruction) was recently found in a "shrine" room in neolithic Çatal Hüyük along with the portrayal of a deer hunt, below. The bull is surrounded by numerous fragmentary figures that apparently represent either hunters or worshipers, and other evidence found at the site suggests that this painting was connected with an early cult. The horns of bulls were preserved at Çatal Hüyük either in small plastered rooms or set in plaster near the hearth, which seems to indicate the beginnings of the bull cult so characteristic of the Near East and the Mediterranean at a later date. The awesomeness of the bull, six feet long in the original, and its great size relative to the figures around it, suggests a mood of veneration rather than a hunting scene.

The deer-hunt mural is especially noteworthy for its acute sense of perspective. Partly stylized and partly naturalistic, the painting achieves a three-dimensional effect through the turned heads of the stags and through a proper rendering of linear perspective in the treatment of the antlers. It also exemplifies a preoccupation with live action that is typical of the Çatal Hüyük murals. At bottom a wounded stag attempts to bolt free from its attackers; at upper right a doe shields its fawn from the pursuing hunters; and at left the leader of the hunt appears ready to cope with any, and all, of the animals missed by the other hunters.

The author of the article on p. 11, James Mellaart, directed the excavations that uncovered the Çatal Hüyük murals and is currently lecturer in prehistoric archaeology at the University of Istanbul.

FROM RECONSTRUCTION BY ANNE LOUISE STOCKDALE

13

By ROBERT BENDINER

The Non-Teachers

They are our new elite of college professors, so busy working for government,

business, foundations, or themselves as to be almost total strangers to the classroom

In the five years since the Russians put Sputnik I into orbit and sent the American demand for brains almost as high, few changes have been as impressive as the swift evolution of the college professor. The popular caricature of absent-minded Academic Man, complete with pipe, shabby suit, and air of genial befuddlement, is swiftly receding into the museum of discarded stereotypes; and in its place is a picture equally exaggerated but equally drawn from reality. From his dusty cocoon the professor has suddenly emerged as consultant, world traveler, diplomat, technician, and television personality. And his metamorphosis, amusing as it may be, has raised the question, voiced in tones of mounting alarm, of just who is to do

the teaching now that he has become a many-splendored thing.

In the large front-rank universities, teaching, at least to undergraduates, has all too clearly been losing ground as a major concern, and the higher a man's standing, the less he has to do with students. For four or five decades university teaching as such has had to contend increasingly with the competitive attractions of research and writing, a bone of contention that we will consider presently. But more recently, with the flood of grants and contracts from government and foundations, the movement of teachers from classroom and lecture hall has become a stampede. When, in addition, the professor finds himself wooed by steel manufacturers ready to pay five hundred dollars a day for his advice on metallurgic short cuts; when South American universities beg his guidance in setting up schools of economics and Asian principalities look to him to train their policemen; when professional organizations sponsored by generous foundations invite him to conferences in Crete or the Vale of Kashmir, all expenses paid, it is not surprising that lecturing to freshmen should have lost much of its appeal. Few, however, put the matter as bluntly as the University of Chicago professor who is said to have observed that the sight of an undergraduate made him ill.

On a big Ivy League campus or at a major state university today, 15 per cent of the faculty are likely at any given time to be off on missions to the ends of the earth. Some institutions now provide an overstaffing of faculty to cover this expected drain, but since it may prove heaviest in departments where it is least expected, preparation is not always possible. The political science department of a large midwestern university recently found itself with more faculty members abroad than on duty and was forced to hire emergency substitutes to teach its students. It is not uncommon, I am told, for eight or nine of the thirty faculty members of the political science department of the University of California at Berkeley to be away and, in the course of a tour this year, I found similar absentee records elsewhere. Edward W. Weidner's recent survey, *The World Role of Universities,* credits American universities with running more than one hundred twenty-five major technical assistance programs abroad, from a Johns Hopkins public health program in Brazil to the University of Indiana's project for training Indonesians in the arts of public administration. And faculty members are, individually, involved in hundreds of others.

The problem that these latter-day peripatetics, not to mention those who have gone into government service, present to college administrations must be staggering. "A university gives a man tenure and the assurance of a lifetime's work," sadly remarks Dean John Perry Miller of the Yale Graduate School. "The question is whether he always recognizes his obligation to the university. A man may ask only a year's leave, but it often turns out to be two or three. Meanwhile, the university has to take on a replacement and give *him* tenure—if it wants quality—and it may find itself in an uncomfortable position when the man on leave wants to return."

For the select of the academic world, however, there is no doubt that dreams of the good life have at last come true. Encountering a new respect in government and industry, earning $30,000 to $40,000 a year between salary and outside consulting, and wooed ardently on all sides, the elite of faculty men have come a long way from the days when "perfessor" was a semicontemptuous term, applied alike to Ph.D.'s, Chautauqua lecturers, and musicians in the burlesque pit. Professor Kenneth E. Eble, of the University of Utah, has put the matter succinctly: "Being long neglected, poorly paid, and retiring by nature, the university professor may be pardoned for acting like a wanton spinster at the first show of worldly interest."

In this favorable position he has been able, first, to lighten appreciably the "teaching load," an expression that would in itself have pained and bewildered Mr. Chips. In the year before World War II began, 15 or 16 class-hours a week was considered reasonable though even then the best universities had reduced the load to 10 or 12 for professors engaged in research. A major report prepared for the Federal government by Dr. Harold Orlans at the Brookings Institution shows that at twelve leading universities today the mean teaching load is 8.3 classroom hours in the humanities and only six in the sciences. At California in Berkeley I was told that, in the jargon of the trade, FTE—"full-time equivalent"—is eight "contact hours" a week with the students but that less than half the faculty actually suffers that much contact. The usual teaching schedule is six hours, and professors who have administrative duties or do graduate teaching may carry no more than three.

Mere mention of the University of Chicago brings a gleam to the academic eye. For there a man may teach one or two courses for two quarters of the year, and enjoy a third quarter without any teaching at all, besides taking the usual three months off in the summer. In short, he teaches either three hours or six hours a week for exactly half the year and is free the rest of the time to write, study, travel, or simply sit. Like faculty men elsewhere, he may choose to put in his time more profitably, of course, on contract to government—Federal, state, or local—or to private industry, provided the work is thought relevant to his discipline. Or again, he may be engaged by one of the foundations to investigate, for good pay, the courting habits of the fruit fly or to account for the erosion of the dative case in English.

At the peak of the profession are those visiting celebrities who can collect a good year's salary for a few lectures a term and otherwise need not appear within a thousand miles of the campus. There are top stars, too, who hold chairs that call for no teaching responsibility at all. And on one campus that I visited there was spirited talk among the faculty of the special lure that had been dangled in front of an eminent colleague: another university, it seems, had offered to start paying him immediately, at the highest salary level, if he would agree to join its staff *two years later.* To the shock of the cynical, he modestly declined on the ground that he would not enjoy life on so high a pedestal.

Where does this professorial flight from the classroom leave the lowly tuition-paying student? In the undergraduate colleges of the great universities it leaves him more and more dependent on Teaching Assistants, or T.A.'s—that is, graduate students who have had little or no training as teachers, whose minds may be largely on their simultaneous pursuit of a master's or doctor's degree, and who may have no intention, once they get it, of having anything further to do with the academic life.

Parents who fondly send their sons to renowned seats of learning expecting them to be taught by the great names listed in the catalogue should shake the dew from their eyes. Assuming the bearers of said names are not off on missions to Upper Volta, Washington, or Macao, they are rarely available personally to undergraduates, except perhaps in a limited way to the cream of upperclassmen. For freshmen, sophomores, and most juniors there is often only the remote contact with professors—usually assistant or associate—in the lecture hall. Otherwise, their mentors are chiefly the T.A.'s, whom they soon learn to look upon contemptuously and who look upon them even more so in return. "Teaching Assistants remind me of hyphenated Americans, who are generally more nationalist than anyone else," Professor Paul Seabury says. "Being young and freshly graduated themselves, they are all the more keen to dissociate themselves from youth."

The undergraduate's loss is not the graduate student's gain

The state of affairs is illuminated by figures from the Orlans report. In the twelve universities receiving the most Federal research money (1960–61), full-fledged professors report putting into undergraduate teaching less than a quarter of their working time. They give graduate students a little more of their time (24.6 per cent), reserving the remaining 52 per cent for research, administration, and other non-teaching activities. For associate professors the working time devoted to undergraduates rises to 31 per cent; for assistant professors, to 39 per cent; but even the lowly instructor is reported as giving no more than 56.5 per cent of his time to the undergraduate. These figures are for all departments. In the sciences alone the breakdown is still more striking, even the mere instructors devoting less than 47 per cent of their time to undergraduate teaching. Responding to a poll, moreover, they expressed a desire to reduce their attentions on this front much further, to a scant 27 per cent.

No wonder, then, that the report describes the undergraduate teaching personnel at the big universities as "mainly young men awaiting advancement, older professors surviving from days when undergraduate teaching was more esteemed, women, foreigners, able but doctorless souls, mediocrities with doctorates, and others who, for one reason or another, belong to the legion of the academically disenfranchised." As an afterthought the author adds that "cases in which influential and productive men like David Riesman or C. Wright Mills have lodged for many years in the undergraduate college of a great university are so rare as to prove the rule."

In the crowded state of these institutions one hardly expects to find Mark Hopkins and a student sharing a bench and a discourse, but the alienation of teacher from students seems to have gone so far that at the top schools studied by Dr. Orlans more than half the faculty could name few or no senior majors in their respective departments. Seniors at some of the best universities did not know any faculty member well enough to produce the references required for a fellowship or a job. And Orlans quotes the graduate dean of Harvard to the effect that in the science departments senior professors hardly know the names of their "section men," that is, their graduate Teaching Assistants, much less those of the students taking their courses.

So runs the broad criticism. Generally speaking, it is not applied to the independent liberal arts colleges, where there are no graduate schools to siphon off the top academic talent and no elaborate research facilities to drain it away from teaching. But these institutions are not unaffected, because the pull of the good professorial life at the top is felt all along the line, and it is increasingly hard for the independent colleges to hold on to their own best men.

It is a criticism, let me say at once, originating in the university faculties themselves, and it is not by any means one that finds swift and general acceptance. On the contrary, the subject of teachers who don't teach is guaranteed to arouse the liveliest polemics in almost any academic gathering.

Probably the most eloquent voice on the offensive is that of Jacques Barzun, Dean of Faculties and Provost of Columbia University. Speaking in Washington last spring, Dr. Barzun voiced appreciation of the world's need for professorial help in setting itself to rights, but enough was enough:

. . . we must be aware that since the last war, outside demands on the university have become a regular bombardment. The distinguished specialists of the university are daily assailed by requests to drop what they are doing and go somewhere to do something which is more or less related to their proper task . . . a scholar who acts as consultant to industry or government will honestly think he is acquiring valuable experience and will become a wiser man and teacher. But there is a point of diminishing returns—the point at which he has to neglect his students in order to get through his consulting. . . . Even now our people are so busy and so distracted, they are beginning to forget what a university is for.

Professor Barzun is not one to underestimate the value of the American university's global contribution, though he does refer with a noticeable edge to demands that it "fix the finances of Ruritania" and "entertain the P.T.A. with free lectures on the beauties of modern art." What he does resent, he makes clear to a questioner, is "the false standard that is being set up, which values research and thinks teaching can be done by most anybody," the notion that "one who remains in teaching is a wallflower who has not been asked to go dancing around on government junkets."

Professor Eble, to whom I have already referred, reinforces the Barzun position with a demand that the "university should be a community of scholars; it should not become a mere way station for commuters." And a professor writing in the New York *Times* Magazine under the frolicsome pen name of John Q. Academicus not long ago attempted thus to put the sponsored researcher in his place:

Clad in the robes of financial ermine, he is the Prince Charming of the faculty, the darling (and at times the spoiled brat) of the administration, and the pride of his department.

Although a member of the teaching staff, *he does not have to teach.* . . . In fact to call a person a good teacher in many leading institutions today is more than damnation by faint praise: it has become almost an academic smear.

To all of which the late Professor Charles A. Fenton of Yale entered in the Association of American University Professors *Bulletin* a reply typical of the extreme defenders of the new dispensation:

The devoted teacher breed has attained a great deal more of the prestige they so childishly value than would have been the case had they settled in the academies where the majority of them more properly belong. . . . It is a pity, however, that the American educational scene, which is necessarily a cloudy one at best, should be made more cloudy by quarter-truths repeated by every shrill, ill-informed, self-elected Mr. Chips.

On a less emotional level the arguments explaining and even promoting the present trend away from teaching are copious and likewise impressive. As so often happens, close examination turns up problems to be solved, a situation to be lived with, rather than culpability to be smoked out. The point was driven home to me in the relaxed environment of Mory's by Yale's Provost, Kingman Brewster, Jr.: "A new competitive market for brains exists. What can you do about it? You can either go on as at present or you can set up separate institutions which are not universities as we know them, but research institutes that have no teaching functions at all. We could make a sharp distinction, as the Germans have, between research institute and university." Like others who are aware of the dilemma, Brewster would stop far short of such a separation, because it is the mixture of research and teaching that gives a university its vitality; he therefore feels there is no alternative to reducing the teaching load if senior faculty men are to be held, against the competition of institutes and private industry, and if juniors are to be attracted in the first place. Significantly, the Orlans report points to the existence, novel in any society, of "a large, permanent, and relatively prosperous corps of doctorate holders outside the academic community." Not just in the physical sciences, either, but also in psychology, economics, and sociology.

Given this outside competition, the university could of course surrender the research function, but would it still be a university? The general formula is that a university has three purposes: to conserve knowledge, through libraries and collections; to disseminate knowledge, by teaching and publishing; and to add to knowledge, through scholarship and research.

If the three objectives were ever or anywhere in perfect proportion, however, they are not so now. The extreme demand for making new advances in knowledge, and the outside money to back up the demand, has drastically shifted the balance to research. However provosts and deans may talk of taking equally into account a man's teaching ability and his scholarship, as revealed by his research and publications, the latter outweighs the former, invariably and often overwhelmingly. Officially, I was told by Professor Peter Odegard, of the political science department at Berkeley, that the official criteria for promotion at his institution include teaching ability, research and publication, professional standing in the discipline at large and, in the case of practitioners like lawyers and doctors, professional competence. But in fact, Odegard says, teaching ability has a weighting of about 10 per cent; standing in the discipline, the same; and professional competence perhaps 5 per cent. This leaves 75 or 80 per cent of the weight on research and publication, and he suggests that the same distribution is true at Harvard, Yale, and Columbia, and not very far off for leading state universities such as Michigan, Wisconsin, Minnesota, and Ohio.

At the American Council of Learned Societies, its president, Dr. Frederick Burkhardt, will tell you that the teaching of undergraduates ranks third as a criterion in some universities, but more often it is fifth or sixth, outranked by publications, prestige, personal qualities, and helpfulness to the institution or the community. The formula I was given at Yale is that, between teaching and scholarship, a man must be good in one and excellent in the other. But in practice, according to Dean William C. De Vane, teaching ability is a factor only in a man's first promotion, after which it is taken for granted.

One reason for the disparity is that you can count the books and articles a man has written, the lecture invitations and grants he has won outside the college, and the number of times he is quoted in the learned journals; but it is extremely difficult to weigh his teaching performance. Unless administrative officials are to spy on him at work as though he were a kindergarten teacher fresh from normal school, which no self-respecting don will allow, no way has yet been found to judge—except, as Dr. De Vane fetchingly admits, "hearsay, pure hearsay."

Away from the classroom and off to the Frontier

Certainly, popularity with students is not an acceptable measuring rod. On the contrary, I was told by Dr. Pendleton Herring of the Social Science Research Council: "To have the reputation of being a great teacher is a dangerous one to acquire. It means that one gets satisfaction from enjoying an appeal to his juniors rather than his peers, that perhaps he is even seeking such popularity. But in the academic world a man must submit to the judgment of his peers, not his juniors. And this can be done only by way of the papers and books he produces. The avuncular role is all very well, but it is far from being enough."

But the mechanical problem of evaluating a man's teaching is less important than the fact that, on this level of education, continuing scholarship is a major *part* of being a good teacher. Dr. Buell Gallagher, President of City College of New York, holds, with many other leading educators, that "nothing *but* classroom teaching can be a deadly thing" and as great a danger as research overstressed at the expense of teaching. Professor Samuel H. Beer of Harvard is even more explicit: "A teacher is not much good unless he is breaking ground, experimenting, advancing in his own discipline. He shares his progress with his students, whom he regards less as students than as other scholars interested in his subject. He can try out his ideas and discoveries with them." If they are not interested enough to share in his work and enthusiasm, let them go their way— that is not the proper concern of the professor.

To the wholly understandable desire of teachers to spend more time in pushing out the frontiers of knowledge there has now been added the enormous incentive of Federal and foundation encouragement, both moral and financial. In its feverish need for technical breakthroughs, the Federal government has become so great a patron of the country's universities that if true peace should suddenly strike from the blue, turmoil on the campus would be almost as great as in the munitions industry. In the year preceding World War II our institutions of higher learning spent no more than $28 million on research, all of it financed by foundations, individuals, and the universities themselves. By 1958, two decades later, they were spending $736 million, with the Federal government footing more than two thirds of the bill. Today the figure is well over a billion, with Washington paying out some $879 million for the work, including the atomic research centers managed by the universities at Los Alamos and Brookhaven. For projects conducted entirely on the campus the Federal government spent $490 million in 1961. At Harvard its contribution accounted for a quarter of the university's entire expenditure, and the Massachusetts Institute of Technology is close to becoming a Federal agency.

While teachers make themselves scarce, students multiply

The simple argument for teachers who have left the classroom to take jobs in Washington, or to do a bit of what the campus cynics describe as "nation-saving" in Kabul or Dakar, is that both teacher and society are the richer for their excursions. At least they should be. Even skeptics like Harry W. Jones, Cardozo Professor of Jurisprudence at Columbia—he has sharply rapped the knuckles of professors who "ride a shuttle service between campus and Washington"—concede that "some taste of the firing line gives depth and dimension to scholarly inquiry." And if we are to stint on letting our professors lend a hand in organizing the schools and public services of struggling young nations, we can expect to suffer a certain opprobrium in the world, not to mention more serious political consequences.

By coincidence these extraordinary demands on our academic resources occur at the very moment when two other factors are subjecting them to severe pressures. First, and too glaring to require emphasis, is the fact that higher education in America has taken on mass dimensions. College enrollments rose 60 per cent in the 1950's and are expected to almost double in the present decade when the great wave of postwar babies reaches college age.

Less obvious is the great increase of graduate students, who demand the attention of the most experienced professors.

Graduate teaching calls for far more preparation than undergraduate and involves keeping up with advances in fields of knowledge that are literally exploding, as well as spending endless time on students' dissertations. Where an instructor can ideally handle fifteen undergraduates in a given course, he is not good for many more than five graduate students. Top scientists in the graduate schools, moreover, have even been known to draw the line at working with doctoral candidates. Only postdoctoral students will do for them.

I have tried to indicate that in the decline of teaching, the problems of the universities are real and the pressures great. But there is reason to believe the problems are more acute than they need be and the pressures less irresistible than they seem. Both government and university could ease matters appreciably with an access of vision in the one and of self-discipline in the other.

Now that it has so enthusiastically embraced higher learning, government would do well, in particular, to distribute its largess more evenly, with a long view to the nation's well-being rather than with an eye solely to the quick technical dividend. Of the more than twelve hundred four-year colleges and universities in the country, one hundred get something like 83 per cent of the Federal funds being doled out for research. Another two hundred scamper for the remaining 17 per cent, and the rest don't even get crumbs. Government research money, moreover, and foundation grants as well, go almost exclusively to graduate schools.

Since this is where experience, facilities, and talent are concentrated, the short-range logic is inescapable, but the consequences of this lopsided spending are nonetheless unhealthy. Inevitably the faculty stars gravitate toward the lush fields of sponsored research, while "slave labor" takes over the teaching of the undergraduates. The process leaves what a forthcoming survey prepared for the Office of Education describes as "islands of neglect," such as those "programs that stimulate, assist, or encourage the students of social progress and human values." In the imbalance created by government and foundation generosity "undergraduate colleges and undergraduate programs in universities which prize the teaching function find it difficult to attract and retain strong faculty members." Only general-purpose grants to the colleges and universities can prevent this warping effect of government aid. To the extent that the state finds valuable these seats of higher learning, it should show its appreciation of all their activities, not merely of the graduate ones, and in that spirit distribute its bounty.

It seems reasonable, on the other hand, to expect the universities themselves to show a greater degree of discrimination, to sanction research projects that break new ground and add to the general knowledge, while rejecting those that merely make for short cuts in the manufacture of nylons, house paint, or even missiles. Professor Barzun compares the current veneration for research, no matter for what, to the medieval attitude toward pilgrimages, conjuring up a droll picture of the teacher fleeing from his students to the protection of the library. Once within he "cries 'research!' as the medieval thief fled to the church and cried 'sanctuary!'"

Other critics, with less imagination, have characterized much of the published research that streams from the presses as "yardage," "foolish and unnecessary," and "the quantification of the obvious." Caplow and McGee, in their scathing *Academic Marketplace,* find "the empty rituals of research . . . practiced with particular zeal in unsuitable fields, so that a published article is regarded as more valuable than skillful teaching [even] in such expedient sciences as mortuary education."

All-out for research and promotion; yet someone is left behind

Some idea of the tidal wave of ink that washes over the profession is conveyed in the revelation of a Yale professor that since the first learned journal appeared in 1665, the number of such publications has increased by a factor of ten every half century. By 1900 there were accordingly ten thousand, and by now we must have in the neighborhood of one hundred thousand, containing unimaginable tons of unassimilated information. Even the abstracts, introduced in 1830 to help solve the problem, are now believed to be increasing at the same rate.

In large part this relentless accumulation of data—from fresh and original to downright insipid—is a consequence of the academic injunction "Publish or perish." It seems not too much to ask, as Professor Odegard suggests, that "more of a distinction should be made between publication and real research." So one-sided has the "productivity" criterion for promotion become that many a professor's prime concern is to be well-represented on his department's annual list of faculty writings, even if he has to pad his claim with book reviews. A story now making the faculty rounds concerns two Roman soldiers at the foot of the Cross. "A great teacher," one of them reflectively observes. "Yes," the other replies with a shrug, "but what did he publish?"

Without minimizing a professor's obligation to extend where he can the frontiers of knowledge, it seems to a number of authorities whom I consulted that the universities could and should make more than they do of teaching as a criterion for advancement. What Caplow and McGee call "the alienation of the university faculty from undergraduate education" is due to the lowered evaluation put upon the teaching function. Much of their unconventional volume is given to revealing excerpts from interviews with 418 anonymous professors, such as this one on the case of a teacher who failed to win a promotion:

. . . it was clear that his really tremendous work with this student group hadn't been weighed at all in the consideration of his promotion. He did a really tremendous job. It caused the rest of us to decide that if this kind of activity was not what was honored—and he'd led them to several national recognitions—then we'd do what was honored . . . sitting in the library and writing weighty papers, and let their god-damned student group go to hell, which it has.

A report of the American Council on Education by John W. Gustad finds the lack of any real method for evaluating college teaching a matter for the "greatest concern." As long as the evaluation is left to the professional societies, with their almost exclusive concern for publication, he says, "pious statements in catalogues about the importance of teaching will be viewed increasingly with a cynical and jaundiced eye by faculty members who know the facts of life."

As for Academic Man's excursion into the wide world of affairs, which nobody can condemn outright, the watchword I encountered everywhere was "self-discipline." The common judgment in the field is that neither men nor institutions have been declining invitations often enough. But when it comes to saying where the line should be drawn, opinion is wide and flexible. I find a bit extreme the injunction of Dr. Jones that "a university's *only* sufficient reason for making its professors available for public service is that they will return better equipped for effective teaching and imaginative scholarship." At the opposite pole is the view of Professor Beer that for some faculty men there is an obligation to spend time in politics or public office, regardless of the demand for their teaching, simply because they are needed in public life. While "politics with only intellectuals would be visionary . . . politics without intellectuals would be visionless."

Somewhere in between is the counsel of Dr. Barzun: "Most universities are working at capacity for the state, for the world, and for posterity. The time has come when we must weigh every new proposal. No pride or false sense of dignity is at work. The university is not afraid of being called a service station when the services are there to be dispensed. But a university has a unique service to perform—to remove ignorance— and it must not allow anybody or anything to distract the institution or its members from that traditional task."

It is a formula not easy to apply, and one that obviously allows a wide latitude for interpretation. But if both institutions and individuals want to invoke it in good faith, they will not find it impossible, I should imagine, to distinguish between research that deals with the narrow, applied, and specific and research that leads to what is conceptually new. They should be able to distinguish a mission that promises to enrich a teacher from one that would merely use him. They should even find it possible to appreciate the war on ignorance waged in the classroom as well as that waged in the library and the laboratory—and to reward it accordingly. As for philosophers in government, the need was never greater, but philosophers are not to be found exclusively on college faculties. And if too many of these leave the campus for the forum, who will be left to teach the philosophers of future governments and the future teachers of philosophers?

Robert Bendiner, a contributor to many national magazines and author of White House Fever, *a book about candidates for the Presidency, was recently awarded a Guggenheim Fellowship to write a study of American political institutions.*

A Memorandum

Chère cousine: Please do not think it strange that I, a sovereign, should thus address you, a republican. Though you and I have lived in worlds apart, I observe that times are changing, and it is with pleasure that I greet in you a kindred spirit, fully deserving of the form of salutation customary among royalty.

While I myself admit to a certain ancestral connection with the United States—my maternal grandfather, William Kirkpatrick, was in his time American consul at Málaga in my native Spain—it is only now that I have come to feel any true rapport with your great nation beyond the sea. The cause of this is entirely yourself. When I learned of the rare charm of your person, the exquisite grace of your presence in the highest place, and the extraordinary influence that you, so youthful, are exerting from there upon the arts and tastes of your compatriots, I realized that we are indeed faced with a new American order of things. And reverberations of your presence and influence are being felt also in Europe and as far east as Moscow—where, I am told, the more enlightened young are making efforts to imitate, for instance, your coiffure.

I had not dreamed that a republic, however powerful, would lead the world in terms of sheer style, and I felicitate you upon setting a *ton* that may enliven and enrich the age.

It was I myself, of course, who last did this, when after the dullness of the July Monarchy and the drabness of the Second Republic I set out at my Emperor's side to restore high taste and elegance to France. How alike we are in many respects: both women artistically inclined from the start (how well I recall Stendhal and Prosper Mérimée, friends of my girlhood), both musical, both patronesses of intellect, makers of new fashion, givers of great festivities, and ardent horsewomen, too!

At the same time, *ma chère*, we have each had our own problems, have we not? One of mine was my husband. What a vacillating and unreliable personality, despite his Napoleonic qualities! I don't think he ever really liked the many intellectuals I brought into our salons: certainly they did not like him, and Victor Hugo and George Sand in particular caused us endless chagrin. In your case, fortunately, the only personal difficulties seem to be with gentlemen of industry—though I would have thought, from both your backgrounds, that there would be no doubt about their

By WILLIAM HARLAN HALE

entrée. I should think that one of your particular problems might be the White House itself. How can you do so much in such limited surroundings? After all, I had in addition to the Tuileries the châteaux of Fontainebleau and Compiègne —both excellent for balls, hunting parties, *fêtes champêtres,* fireworks, charades, etc.—not to speak of Versailles and Saint Cloud. But you, what do you have when you wish to change the scene? Hyannisport!

As for myself, moreover, I found that when one embarks upon a program of setting taste, attracting an elite, beautifying the capital, and generally encouraging arts and cultivated manners, one must be able to enforce it. For this purpose I had at hand a Court, as obedient to me as to the Emperor; the French Academy, the election of whose "immortals" I could influence; Ministers of State beholden to me; and the Emperor himself, who often deferred to me on such matters as Baron Haussmann's redesign of Paris or the additions to the Louvre, particularly when off on his wars or preoccupied with our fiasco in Mexico (the predecessor of your own in Cuba). Did old Prosper Mérimée covet a seat in the Senate? I arranged it. Did Rosa Bonheur (probably not one of your favorite painters) aspire to the Légion d'honneur? I helped arrange that, too. If I could offer you any advice, it would be to consolidate your position—and use it. I insisted on a place in the Council of Ministers, and in my husband's absence even served as Regent. And when that upstart Bismarck and his King William of Prussia visited Paris shortly before 1870 to get a taste of supposedly decadent French culture, who let them feel its steel? I did. Those *boches!* Then they turned around and started that war.

But you, *ma chère,* hold none of these attributes of might. And I am told that for all your present influence you remain the insouciant person you were when you entered upon your near-regal role—independent, original, and with no Establishment of your own to make your decisions as arbiter of an era's taste *de rigueur.* I tremble for you. The opposition may undermine you. Yet perhaps you find more joy in your role than I did in mine. For despite all my efforts, the opposition eventually threw out Napoleon III and myself, too, and the thankless French seem to remember me chiefly as the leading wearer of a once-stylish hat. I observe that you often omit hats.

DRAWINGS BY DAVID LEVINE

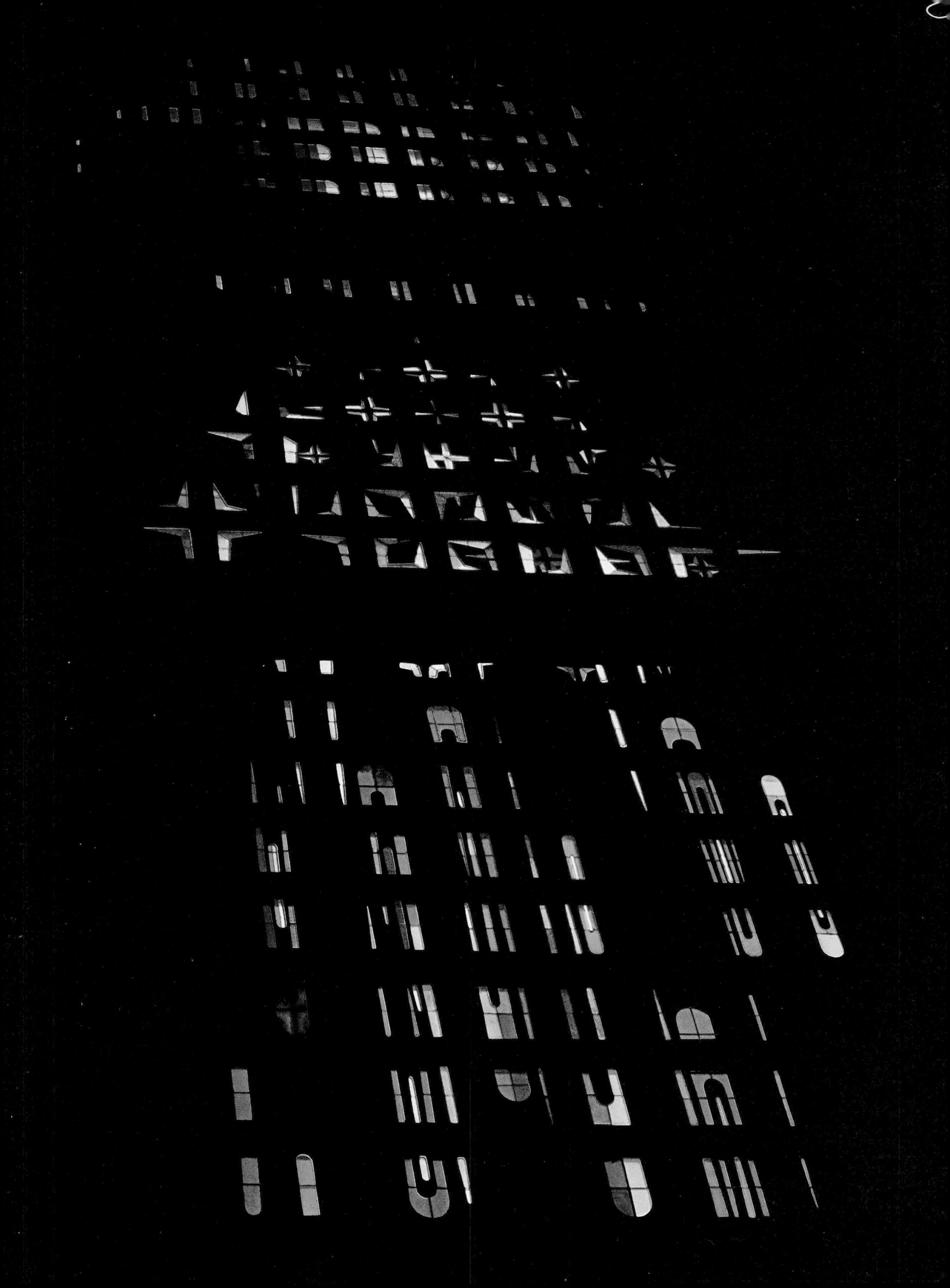

Opposite: Pinpoints of pure color (fifty-two different shades) create bright, staccato rhythms along the upper walls of the church of St. Rémy at Baccarat, France. The window designers achieved this effect by setting small geometric shapes of Baccarat crystal in a waffle-like concrete grid. The church itself, of raw reinforced concrete, was designed by Nicolas Kazis and completed in 1957.

THROUGH THE GLASS BRIGHTLY

New churches abroad glow with the richest light since the Middle Ages

Until very recently most of us assumed that only medieval artists and craftsmen were capable of creating great art in stained glass. Though their world was even darker, we said, their faith shone more vividly than ours.

Secular enlightenment since the Middle Ages may, indeed, have dimmed religious expression. But stained glass has had a startling revival in the past few years, and to its many admirers much of the new glass seems as devout as that of the cathedrals. As in Gothic times, it is not an isolated art, destined for the collector or museum, but an intrinsic part of a new religious architecture. Its finest examples have been created by some of the most celebrated artists of the day to enhance small churches for ordinary people in ordinary, out-of-the-way places.

Though the technique remains largely traditional, the design of the revived art has radically broken with tradition. The windows of the twelfth and thirteenth centuries—such as those at Chartres, Sens, St. Denis, or Canterbury—proclaimed the Christian message in touchingly literal pictures, but the best of twentieth-century windows and glass walls are mainly abstract or abstracted. The medium, with its resolute outlines and barbaric richness of color, invites the bold forms of modern expression. Yet the message is also unmistakably spiritual and often as moving as the Gothic images. The new stained glass, too, has the same power to shut out the workaday world and to transfigure the space it adorns.

Stained glass first appeared in the cathedrals of Augsburg and Le Mans some nine hundred years ago. It was a sudden birth in full-blown glory. There seems to have been no gradual evolution of the art, no prelude. Glass, of course, and colored glass as well, had been used for centuries before. But a pictorial design of colored glass—a translucent mosaic, as it were—seems to have been the instant inspiration of an unknown genius. And it, in turn, helped to inspire new structures that strove to accommodate larger and larger expanses of stained glass.

The decline of the art began when the mystic semidarkness of the Gothic cathedrals gave way to the Renaissance light of learning and humanism. The architect now predominated, and embellished his work with gilded splendor, soft frescoes, and bright marble. Though Italian, Spanish, and Flemish Renaissance masters still created stained-glass windows, they regarded them as huge transparent canvases on which they "painted" in more elaborate technique and ever lighter hues, but with lessened emotional impact.

The new rational spirit did the rest. The Puritans in England, as did the Lutherans in Germany, actually destroyed many glorious medieval windows, which rivaled those of France. A Puritan minister of Canterbury gleefully related how he stood high on a ladder with a pike and "rattled down proud Beckett's glassie bones." In Catholic France, too, the blue and ruby "gloom" of the old cathedrals fell out of favor, and both buildings and windows were sadly neglected.

It was a nineteenth-century change in taste that helped the craft to survive: the Gothic revival. One result, when it crossed the Channel from England, was that the French be-

23

By WOLF VON ECKARDT

gan to restore their medieval monuments. As part of this process, the French government gave encouragement to small stained-glass workshops in many parts of the country, so that they could replace and restore cathedral windows. And when French artists revived the art of stained glass after World War II, the craftsmen were able to respond with skill and enthusiasm.

Just what prompted the current stained-glass revival is difficult to pin down precisely. The need to rebuild the churches destroyed or damaged in World War II—four thousand in France alone—may have had something to do with it in the beginning. Certainly the passionate efforts of Father M.-A. Couturier to revitalize Christian art helped importantly to encourage it. This French Dominican priest, who had studied art in his youth and was disgusted with the pastiche decoration of most recent churches, fought hard for permission to enlist famous and brazenly modern painters in his cause, regardless of their faith or conviction. His first accomplishment was Notre-Dame de Toute-Grâce at Assy, in the shadow of Mont Blanc, begun in 1937 and completed in 1950. Maurice Novarina was the architect; Fernand Léger, Jean Lurçat, Germaine Richier, Marc Chagall, and Jacques Lipchitz all contributed their talents to this church, and Georges Rouault designed some of the stained-glass windows. Among the clergy Father Couturier's efforts are still hotly debated, both on grounds of taste and theology, but his influence on contemporary liturgical art is already strongly felt throughout the Western world. One of its fruits is the rejuvenation of stained glass.

Most of the new designers employ the old methods. The glass is "stained" by various metallic oxides, either added in the molten state or applied to the surface of the glass before refiring. It is made into panes that are often delightfully rough and textured. These are cut to the designer's cartoon and joined with strips of lead, grooved on two sides, which in cross section look like the letter H. These "cames," as they are called, are soldered where they join. Since the soft lead could not even support its own weight, let alone the pressure of wind, the window is reinforced by iron bars anchored in the frame.

Marc Chagall, in his blazing windows for the Hadassah-Hebrew University Medical Center at Jerusalem (see pages 26–27), has made particularly ingenious use of the black cames and heavy bars to denote the semiabstract design of his animals and objects and to emphasize the brilliance of his colors. To add detail, he followed the medieval practice of painting on the glass with a brownish enamel, called grisaille, before refiring in the kiln. Like the Gothic artists, Chagall used grisaille sparingly; its overuse since the Renaissance helped to ruin the simple beauty of the medium. To shade his colors, Chagall borrowed still another technique from the Middle Ages: the use of "flashed glass," which consists of thin films fused together. Layer by layer the films are then chipped, ground, or eaten away by acid.

Heinz Bienefeld dispensed with these refinements in his far more muted stained-glass wall for the church of St. Mary the Queen outside Cologne, and relied entirely on color and abstract pattern (see pages 30–31). His wall, like most of the new stained glass, integrates his art with the structure.

A new method developed quite recently by French craftsmen, notably Gabriel Loire of Chartres, was used in Father Couturier's second triumph—the church of Sacre Coeur at Audincourt, a drab industrial town near the Swiss border (see opposite). Faceted chunks of colored glass, up to an inch thick, are set in a special cement and are thus self-supporting. The technique is variously called *betonglas* or *dalle de verre*. The church itself, designed by Novarina and immeasurably enhanced by Fernand Léger's stained-glass girdle around its U-shaped bulk, is neither traditional nor avant-garde. It is given distinction and a marvelous interior surprise by its baptistry, a small, round pavilion that stands near the front façade, a little away from the building but connected to it by a short corridor. Both passage and corridor walls, from floor to ceiling, are entirely of *betonglas* in a design by the painter Jean Bazaine. On the outside these walls are strongly patterned like some strange, new marble, while the interior is enveloped in jeweled light.

A team of four designers, working with the architect Nicolas Kazis, has achieved a crisper, more rhythmic effect in the church of St. Rémy at Baccarat, a center of French glassmaking (see page 22). Here small pieces of colored glass are set deep into sculptured molds of concrete, adding the play of shadow to their colored light.

Alfred Manessier's windows at Hem, near Lille, also use the thick, faceted, colored glass that has been quickly accepted by modern church architects (see page 28). In the United States it was first seen in the First Presbyterian Church at Stamford, Connecticut, where the architect Wallace K. Harrison carried it even higher than in the Audincourt baptistry—to the very top of his tentlike structure.

What has become the biggest religious building boom ever, caused not only by the devastation of World War II in Europe but also by the population changes on both sides of the Atlantic, gives further impetus to the stained-glass revival. Yet the most decisive stimulant of the new art in the old medium is, undoubtedly, modern church architecture. Its radical break with tradition seems to demand new forms of artistic expression.

Or was it that the artists themselves insisted on bringing their color and emotion to these cold, monochromatic structures? *"Donnez-moi des murs!"* (give me walls), the painter Léger, tired of confining canvases, had cried in the thirties. Now there are opportunities aplenty. Artists, architects, and craftsmen are collaborating on stained-glass walls that form as well as adorn the new spaces of worship. It was thus when the old cathedrals were built.

Wolf Von Eckardt is the author of the article on the Bauhaus that appeared in the November, 1961, issue of HORIZON.

Floor-to-ceiling windows of betonglas (chunks of colored glass set in a concrete mastic) turn the baptistry of the church of Sacre Coeur at Audincourt (1952), in eastern France, into a glowing cage of light (seen from the outside, at right; from within, below). These windows were designed by the painter Jean Bazaine, and the long clerestory window in the church proper by Fernand Léger. The architect was Maurice Novarina.

The set of twelve big windows designed by Marc Chagall for the synagogue of the new Hadassah-Hebrew University Medical Center at Jerusalem is already being acclaimed as the supreme achievement of his career. Unlike most contemporary stained glass, Chagall's windows are not abstract. Each symbolizes one of the twelve tribes of Israel—not with human figures, since Jewish tradition forbids them in religious art—but with images of birds, animals, fishes, and flowers drawn partly from the Old Testament and partly from the iconography of Chagall's own painting. At the left are two preliminary sketches for the tribe of Naphtali, described in Genesis 49:21 as "a hind let loose," and opposite is the window as it was executed. They were completed in 1961, and have since been installed in the arches of the lantern, or raised portion, of the synagogue (below).

The Chagall reproductions on these pages and on HORIZON's cover will appear in the book The Jerusalem Windows of Marc Chagall, to be published in October by George Braziller in association with this magazine. The text is by the French critic Jean Leymarie, and there are 105 plates—66 in full color—showing every stage of Chagall's masterwork from his earliest sketches to the finished windows.

Left: Bold windows of blue, white, and gold alternate with slabs of plain red brick in the accordion-pleated walls of Christ Church at Bochum, Germany. They cast their light toward the altar. The church, which replaces one destroyed in World War II, was designed by Dieter Oesterlen, with glass by Helmut Landir.

Below: Not windows but an entire "wall of light" was created by the painter Alfred Manessier for this small chapel at Hem, France. Though abstract, the progression of colors—from palest shades through deep reds and blues to gold—was intended to symbolize the various stages of the life of Saint Thérèse of Lisieux.

Right: Francis Bott made extensive use of grisaille—the technique of painting the glass before refiring it—to create a more "painterly" type of window for the chapel of the Château de Reux in Normandy. The style is contemporary, but the windows themselves—of which this is a center panel—are Gothic in shape.

Overleaf: The austere, boxlike church of St. Mary the Queen in the outskirts of Cologne is given unexpected magnificence by a south wall entirely of glass. Designer Heinz Bienefeld's greenish-gray palette and leafy shapes seem to bring the woods into the church. The doorway leads to a baptistry in the same style.

This simple but dramatic window was designed by the late Father Couturier in 1948 for a Dominican chapel in Le Havre. His greatest achievement, however, was to enlist the talents of France's foremost painters and sculptors in the creation of new religious art—a movement that has revitalized the decoration and design of churches almost everywhere in the Western world.

Making a Cult of Confusion

The new Theatre of the Absurd dwells on ambiguity, chaos, irrelevance. But how irrelevant can you get, if you say your meaning is to have no meaning at all?

Oddly enough, ambiguity is a quality that has often been admired in the theatre. It is not a quality anyone can let alone, even when he professes to admire it. The character of Hamlet, we say, is ambiguous. Is Hamlet a man of action or a man incapable of action? More than 350 years of grappling have not resolved the issue; neither have they quieted the demon that keeps urging us to try to resolve it. The implications of *King Lear* are ambiguous: Whose fault is it that Lear's children treat him as they do? Alceste, Molière's misanthrope, is ambiguous: In demanding that society behave more honorably than it does, is he right, is he ridiculous, or is he both right and ridiculous? We do probe as though it were essential to us to know the answers.

Yet even as we probe we recognize that the very mystery that has so far defeated us is in some measure responsible for the greatness of the play. We sense that, no matter what "ambiguities" may tease us on the face of things, we are nevertheless in the presence of an ultimate, existential clarity, an intuited clarity of the core, that untouchable center—infinitesimal and red-hot—which sends its rays outward in intangible wave-lengths to lave, with the same slant of light, a half-dozen surfaces that in themselves appear irreconcilable. We are making our way through a multidimensional reality across which a complex of veils is constantly playing, throwing now this side and now that into surprising relief, toward a solid that is implied at the center; and the combined sensations of evanescence and solidity correspond nicely to the yes-and-no, now-you-see-it-and-now-you-don't lives we lead. The degree to which a play is ambiguous, but

Often the works of "absurd" playwrights appear to be not so much plays as a series of dramatic double exposures. This assembly of bewitched, bothered, and bifocal characters from the avant-garde canon, drawn by Douglas Gorsline for HORIZON, *includes, from left to right: Mac Davis, the unwashed wanderer—from Harold Pinter's* The Caretaker; *a bank clerk posing as a judge and an athletic pimp playing an executioner—from Jean Genet's* The Balcony; *a grandmother dying beside the ocean—from Edward Albee's* The Sandbox; *three masked-and-cloaked Negroes imitating white men—from Genet's* The Blacks; *Hamm, a wheel-chair philosopher (in multidimensional sunglasses), and his man of all work, Clov (in a knotted nightcap)—from Samuel Beckett's* Endgame; *the empty-headed adolescent who is Albee's wry conception of* The American Dream; *Zero Mostel as John, in Eugène Ionesco's play* Rhinoceros; *a nymphet heroine (who turns into a seductress) and a timorous hero (who turns into a killer)—from Arthur Kopit's* Oh Dad, Poor Dad, Mamma's Hung You in the Closet and I'm Feelin' So Sad; *and, poking up from the scenery in the lower right-hand corner, an enfeebled ancient who is the entire cast of Beckett's* Krapp's Last Tape.

knowable in and through its ambiguity, is often the measure of our affection and respect for it.

In what sense is this also true, or should it be true, of that most deliberately ambiguous of all theatres, the twentieth-century avant-garde form which has come to be called The Theatre of the Absurd? Certainly the plays of Samuel Beckett, Eugène Ionesco, Harold Pinter, Edward Albee, N. F. Simpson, Jean Genet, and Arrabal have not at once capitalized upon our instinctive admiration for the indeterminate, though satisfying, image. Pinter's *The Caretaker* was given an impeccable production last season on Broadway, and met with an enthusiasm in the press that ought to have guaranteed it substantial audiences for a lengthy run. The production did not find those

audiences; the pre-interested attended for a few moderately lively weeks, and the houses dwindled rapidly thereafter. Such examples of the form as have achieved "long" runs—Jean Genet's *The Balcony* and *The Blacks,* the double bill of Samuel Beckett's *Krapp's Last Tape,* and Edward Albee's *The Zoo Story*—have generally done so in off-Broadway playhouses that restrict their capacities to 299 seats.

At the same time, and just as certainly, the form cannot be dismissed as a mere temporary aberration, irrelevant to the atmosphere in which audiences as well as playwrights live; it has already demonstrated too much fecundity for that. In a very few years—ten at the most—it has not only captured the loyalty of genuinely talented writers during their most pro-

ductive time of life, it has leapfrogged its way from country to country and from continent to continent, displaying the power to proliferate though not yet the power to compel the large-scale assent that has sometimes welcomed a degree of obscurity in the past. Is there some essential difference between the un-certainties we grant *The Misanthrope* and the uncertainties we resist in *The Caretaker?*

The Theatre of the Absurd, which is likely to retain that generic label now that Martin Esslin has effectively formalized it in the first full-length study anyone has made of this fairly diversified school of playmaking, is so thoroughly soaked in ambiguity as to seem, upon acquaintance, composed of noth-ing else. The mathematical formulas upon which the universe

may be thought to rest—numbers themselves—are ambiguous in Ionesco's *The Lesson:*

". . . Here are three matches. And here is another one, that makes four. Now watch carefully—we have four matches. I take one away, now how many are left?"

"Five. If three and one make four, four and one make five."

The words with which we describe to one another our knowl-edge of the universe are ambiguous in nearly all such plays, as they are in this Joyce-inspired passage from Beckett's *Waiting for Godot:*

". . . the practise of sports such as tennis football running cycling swimming flying floating riding gliding conating ca-mogie skating tennis of all kinds dying flying sports of all sorts autumn summer winter winter tennis of all kinds hockey of all sorts penicilline and succedanea in a word I resume. . . ."

Whenever we wish to use words as tools of reason, as soldiers in a syllogism designed to prove one or another proposition about the universe, the proof also becomes ambiguous. Thus, in Arrabal's *The Automobile Graveyard:*

"What a brain! And you know how to prove things, like the big shots?"

"Yeah, I have a special method for that. Ask me to prove something for you, something real hard."

"All right, prove me that giraffes go up in elevators."

"Let's see. Giraffes go up in elevators . . . because they go up in elevators."

"God, that was great! . . . Suppose I asked you to prove giraffes *don't* go up in elevators."

"That's easy. I just prove the same thing, but the other way around."

If the insubstantiality of digits, words, syntax, and logic tends to make all communication between people at the very least ambiguous, people are ambiguous as well. An old couple, married or not married, childless or parents of a son, speak constantly at cross-purposes in Ionesco's *The Chairs:*

". . . Where is my mamma? I don't have a mamma anymore."

"I am your wife, I'm the one who is your mamma now."

"That's not true, I'm an orphan, hi, hi."

"My pet, my orphan, dworfan, worfan, morphan, orphan."

* * *

"We had one son . . . he's gone away . . . he was seven years old, the age of reason, I called after him: 'My son, my child, my son, my child.' . . . He didn't even look back . . ."

"Alas, no . . . no, we've never had a child . . . I'd hoped for a son. . . ."

Crucial actions performed by the characters may mean one thing, or another. The climax of Beckett's *Happy Days* is reached when a husband, in frock coat and top hat, crawls on hands and knees to the foot of a mound of sand in which his wife is buried to her neck. A revolver is "conspicuous to her right on mound." With painful effort, the husband attempts to claw his way up the mound. "Oh I say, this is terrific!" cries the wife, certain he is coming to offer her one last kiss. During a pause, doubt crosses her mind. "Is it me you're after, Willie . . . or is it something else?" She does not look at the revolver; Willie does not reach the top of the mound; the play ends without our knowing whether Willie wished to kill himself or kiss his wife (or kill his wife).

The new play of ambiguity is apt to take place in "A bare interior" or on a stage possessing "No décor" during "A late evening in the future." The printed instructions to the stage director may be optional: "The clock strikes as much as it likes." There is ambiguity before the curtain has gone up, ambiguity in rehearsal: "He either kisses or does not kiss Mrs. Smith."

Now the open meanings we are cataloguing here are ob-

viously different from the fluid ambiguities of character and narrative implication we so highly prize in certain plays of the past. At first sight the difference may seem a mere matter of quantity. Hamlet possesses a few ambiguities that are titillating in a world composed mainly of plain statement; here *everything* is unnamed, down to the last detail of stage management, and apparently nothing is at any time intended to be absolute.

Curiously, this is not the case. While vast portions of the familiar world are being steadily atomized in the avant-garde play, and while the familiar tools that help us deal with it are being cumulatively mocked, certain aspects of our residence in the universe are being cast in concrete in such a dense and literal way as to make the dramatic statement seem almost simple-minded. For instance, environment may generally be left vague. But the effect that a given playwright thinks environment may have on us is not left vague at all. It is bill-postered. Suppose it is a playwright's intention to show us that, no matter how free the human animal thinks it is, the human animal is irretrievably earth-bound. Is there any ambiguity, or even any slight subtlety, in presenting us with a woman choked in sand up to the neck? Suppose one wishes to dwell upon the ruthless discard into which the aged or maimed are thrown. In *Endgame* Beckett deposits an elderly couple in ash bins, downstage left. Plainness could not speak better for itself. Suppose a dramatist wishes to convey to us the notion that our once-efficient world has broken down? When he composes his *mise-en-scène* of a disconnected stove, a frame without a picture in it, a rusty lawn mower, a collection of empty suitcases, a rolled-up rug, yesterday's yellowed newspapers, a toaster with a broken plug, and then covers the litter over with a noisily leaking roof—as Pinter has done in *The Caretaker*—he is leaving very, very little to chance.

Ironically, there is far less ambiguity—and, indeed, far less complexity—in each of these illustrations than there would have been if identical attitudes had been incorporated into much more conventional plays. It is possible to suggest that a woman is earth-bound even while she is moving rapidly and gracefully about an expansive living room, as it is possible to imply that the elderly are being discarded even when they are being coddled, or that the world is showing a fissure although the kitchen sink is functioning. We should not see the "truth" as readily, of course; we should have to dig beneath the surface for what is not at all obvious; catching a hint of the interior content, we should have to be willing to continue to look at the play on two levels, although it is generally The Theatre of the Absurd that asks for attention at two levels. In this sense our present avant-garde drama is not so much fluid as fixed.

There are other things that might lead one to question the degree of ambiguity actually present in what is sometimes called anti-drama. The length of the plays is one of them, the recurrence of themes another. Logically speaking, whatever is truly ambiguous ought to require a longer time for its development than whatever is truly plain. Either Yes or No can be said more rapidly than Yes *and* No. Yet some avant-garde plays take as little as eight minutes to perform (one of the most attractive, Edward Albee's *The Sandbox*, cannot take more than twelve or thirteen). Though Beckett, Ionesco, Pinter, and Genet have all written "full-length" plays, only those of Genet seem to demand the running time allotted to a conventional evening in the theatre. Playwrights of the genre have developed a somewhat standard defense of their miniaturism. "What *is* a full-length play?" becomes the riposte. "A play has achieved its full length when it has said what it had to say," even if it has said what it had to say in twenty or twenty-four minutes. Reasonable enough. Still, reasonable or no, what the tendency toward brevity cannot help but suggest is that the premise upon which such a play rests possesses neither the complexity nor the many-sidedness requiring an extended examination under a variety of lights and shadows. (Thus Albee's longish *The American Dream*, interesting as it is, is not more interesting than *The Sandbox*, which it resembles; it runs the obvious risk of belaboring a theme that has earlier been delicately, and perhaps adequately, intimated.) Extreme compactness is the sign of simple, rather than multiple, statement.

Equally strange is the prevalence of a handful of repeated themes. The difficulty, or the impossibility, of communication between people is demonstrated so often as to become a badge of the school. The incrusting effects of conformity are discussed nearly as frequently; most often herd behavior is simply satirized, as in *Rhinoceros*, but sometimes, as in Jack Gelber's *The Apple*, an invitation is issued to cease being square and go far out: "Come over to our side. You're not doing anything important." Closely related to the repeated theme of incrustation is the equally repeated theme of loss of identity. People make so many conventional gestures that they forget, or never have time to discover, what a truly personal gesture might be: "You don't know who you are until you're dead."

And when the interior emptiness that is loss of identity is coupled with the exterior pressure of incrustation—when our habits and the universe harden about us—we find ourselves in the "zero" world that Samuel Beckett creates again and again (as do his imitators). Imprisonment in a chair, in a room, in a sandbank, becomes the familiar point of departure; the act of waiting, for nothing that ever arrives or for something that proves not to have been worth waiting for when it does arrive, becomes the familiar line of tension; either gibberish or a view of the void becomes the not unexpected summation of the essentially static situation. Having seen Beckett's *Endgame*, and having watched an old man climb to a window, put a telescope to his eye, and report that he sees "Nothing . . . nothing," one is entirely prepared to follow a young man as he goes to a window, puts a telescope to his eye, and reports that "there's nothing out there to see" in the youthful Arthur L. Kopit's *Oh Dad,*

Poor Dad, Mamma's Hung You in the Closet and I'm Feelin' So Sad. Echoes scamper from play to play, and sometimes coalesce to make a single play a kind of countinghouse of themes. But when one has counted off the problem of communication, the problem of incrustation, the problem of identity, and the problem of the surrounding void, one is surprised to discover he has more than five fingers left over.

Perhaps it is the combination of these last two odd qualities —shortness of form and familiarity of point—that creates a further impression of essential literalness in much of the work of the avant-garde. The Theatre of the Absurd is generally theatre in a state of shock; it also means, by its methods, to shock those who attend it. But there are occasions when its shock is not the bewilderment of the adult confronted by too much that is eluding him, but the shock of a child who has just now noticed the obvious and is shrilly calling it to our attention. In many plays, for instance, much is made of the fact that words are slippery, unstable tools, not to be trusted as tokens of true meaning. But the proposition, which is offered excitedly, is scarcely as earth-shaking as all that. If the instability of words had not always been evident, no one would ever have been tempted to make a pun, a pun being mankind's playful admission that the words he uses are notoriously unreliable. It is doubtful, indeed, that without this awareness anyone could have conceived the possibility called poetry. For poetry makes its whole effect out of the absence of an absolute value in words: if the word "fire" signified only and absolutely the specific chemical activity of oxidization, Yeats could not so much as write "a fire was in my head."

As we begin to notice that certain propositions put forth in this "new" drama are not entirely novel, we notice something else: the statement of such propositions is remarkably unambiguous. If a playwright composes an unintelligible sentence in order to say that words are unintelligible, he is being utterly straightforward. The line "such caca, such caca, such caca, such caca, such caca, such caca, such caca, such caca, such caca" does not give us a choice of meanings. It confines us to a single, simple, unsupple assertion that there is no meaning. In short what is being said is being said baldly.

But what kind of theatre is this that it should, in spite of all that we feel to be intangible about it, insist upon so much frozen precision, so much explicit illustration, at the surface? It is, in essence, a philosopher's rather than a poet's theatre. For it is the philosopher who needs to make as rigid as possible the external terms in which he clothes his thought. Each term in his hypothesis must mean one thing and no other; the center of his syllogism dare not be undistributed; he does not wish to be guilty of "loose thought." The philosopher deals in defined, and hence hardened, concepts. The poet, historically, works another way. He begins not with an immaterial concept but with a material fragment of nature embodied in a ready-made

The raffish settings of "absurd" plays are bounded by blank walls, decayed scaffolding, and doorways that open onto the unknown; they are crowded with the paraphernalia of poverty, which is supposed to stand for the spiritual malaise of our times, and populated by grotesque beings. Some of these are (left to right): an old woman and her spouse who dwell in a pair of adjacent ash cans and who are the parents of the leading character in Beckett's Endgame; *Krapp, also Beckett's invention, who inhabits a dingy attic in an unspecified location—he is seen here clutching his tape-recorded memorial of youthful love adventures, with which he nostalgically communes; Winnie, a lady (both with and without glasses) half-buried in a mound of sand, which does not inhibit her conversation at all—from Beckett's* Happy Days; *peering down on her, a wife-murderer in an antiseptic jail cell in Jack Richardson's* Gallows Humor, *an uneasy gentleman who is presented with a prostitute by the considerate prison authorities, to lighten his final hour before execution; and finally a swim-suited young man who materializes on a New York beach and represents The Angel of Death (or is he The Angel of Mercy?) in Edward Albee's one-act play* The Sandbox.

musculature of its own, over which he is able to throw a loose-fitting robe that partially conceals and partially reveals. The looseness will suggest something of the form beneath it; but it will not constrict it or keep it from moving freely under its own supple laws.

A philosopher's theatre dare not let its terms be uncertain: these must be fiercely exact so as to lead us, without error, toward the nub of the play's thought, toward that interior pin point upon which its theorem rests. We move by plain paths—along which discarded people repose in ash cans and earthbound women are bound in earth—to the pith of the matter. But, much to our consternation, it is precisely here that we come face to face with a genuine ambiguity, perhaps with the one true ambiguity belonging to The Theatre of the Absurd.

What—behind the bold assertions of the surface—do the plays mean? Pinpointed, what theorem does the philosopher-playwright wish to demonstrate? Two obvious and incompatible answers present themselves.

One is that we have foolishly allowed ourselves to fall into our present state and need to be jolted out of it. We have used words carelessly, or without awareness of their inherent imperfection, and have frustrated our efforts at communication. We have permitted our habits, and our conventional social responses, to form crusts about us. We have forgotten who we are, mislaid our identities. We had better look at these things—hard—and try to correct them before the world breaks down.

The other answer is that, far from being responsible for what has happened to us, we are just now waking up to the fact that nothing we can do, or have done, is capable of affecting the incoherent and immobile nature of the universe. However things are, that is the way they *are*, and forever will be. Communication *is* impossible, as incrustation is inevitable. Identity is an illusion: it exists only on the driver's license that is somewhere in our wallet, and the wallet is lost. It is no use knocking one's head against the universe to prove that one has a head: the universe is not there. The situation cannot be rectified, only recognized.

The avant-garde play of the present time does not give one or the other of these answers; it gives both, or neither. The two positions are maintained, or refused, simultaneously. This ambivalence is not simply something we feel as we sit in the playhouse. It is in the work; in some documented cases it is in the playwright.

Ionesco has explained on one occasion that the "clichés, empty formulas, and slogans" of social life and social thought must be "relentlessly split apart in order to find the living sap beneath." On another occasion the same playwright has defined the subject of his play *The Chairs* as "the absence of people, the absence of the emperor, the absence of God, the absence of matter, the unreality of the world, metaphysical emptiness. The theme of the play is *nothingness*."

On the one hand, a living sap; on the other, nothing.

It is the yes-no of these two mutually contradictory positions, I think, that most often unsettles us in the theatre, sometimes whetting our appetites for more and more of the destructive work that is being done, sometimes defeating us utterly. As long as we seem to see the destructive work as a clearing away of rotted superstructures, with the promise or at least the possibility that new foundations may be laid, the appetite surges. Yes, it is time for examinations of conscience, and the exploration of fresh terrain, at every turn of our lives.

Listening with this one ear, we seem to hear prospects for the future: in announcing plans for a festival of Absurd plays, the producer Richard Barr insisted that the plays offer "a distorted picture of a world that has gone mad" in order to "break the old mold of language and narrative sequence in the theatre and to emphasize its mystery and truth."

It is this same hopeful instinct that leads one to pursue an obviously honest writer along paths that one fears may be blind alleys. Let us say that Harold Pinter wishes to speak—not in a play but in a short story—of the chilling abstractness and indeterminateness of our lives, of the ease with which identity blurs and roles are reversed. Because Mr. Pinter is a conscientious craftsman and in earnest, and because new tools are needed for the tasks, one reads on, fascinated:

When we began, I allowed him intervals. He expressed no desire for these, nor any objection. And so I took it upon myself to adjudge their allotment and duration. They were not consistent, but took alternation with what I must call the progress of our talks. With the chalk I kept I marked the proposed times upon the blackboard, before the beginning of a session, for him to examine, and to offer any criticism if he felt so moved. But he made no objection, nor, during our talks, expressed any desire for a break in the proceedings. However, as I suspected they might benefit both of us, I allowed him intervals.

The story proves to be readable; its conclusion, a few pages and one dissolved world later, is most effective. Still, one gropes one's way through a world that has grown faceless—a world in which there is not so much "chalk" or "blackboard" as there are "times," "intervals," "allotment and duration"—on the assumption that space is being emptied out so that one day it will be clean enough to receive and house a face again. The assumption, however, is not necessarily valid. Pinter may be saying that there are no faces, only "intervals" of a certain "duration" in which "proceedings" take place.

We may be looking into the "*nothingness*" Ionesco asks for, or part way into it. Ionesco insists that in any production of *The Chairs* "the invisible elements must be more and more clearly present, more and more real (to give unreality to reality one must give reality to the unreal), until the point is reached—inadmissible, unacceptable to the reasoning mind—when the unreal elements speak and move." At this point, "nothingness can be heard, is made concrete."

Should this point be reached in actual production, no appetite can stir: there is "nothing" to stir it. If the audience mind has

successfully joined the playwright in an act of cerebration that denies the value of the act of cerebration, if it agrees that the playwright has finally communicated the impossibility of communicating, it has indeed reached "zero," the ultimate impasse. It has contradicted the equipment that permits it to recognize contradictions; it has denied the premises by which it can know premises; it has canceled out the possibility of making any sort of response, because there is nothing to respond to and the very act of responding would itself be gratuitous, irrelevant, insane. When and if the play achieves Ionesco's stated objective for it, the audience mind can only clap down over itself, subside into black silence and never be heard from again. When the play does not achieve this objective, it must be dismissed as a failure: any response it now provokes must be negative, dissatisfied.

A question thrusts its way in here. *Is* it possible to communicate the impossibility of communicating? If the experience cannot, in fact, be realized, then the play is unproducible to begin with. There are indications within Ionesco's own work that this is the case, and that Ionesco—in his interior consistency—is aware of the problem. When he writes in a stage direction, "The clock strikes as much as it likes," he is waiving the possibility of any two performances of the play producing exactly the same effect; he is saying that a defined goal is unreachable. But he goes beyond this waiver. When he writes, "He either kisses or does not kiss Mrs. Smith," he is abandoning the possibility that the play, *as he wrote it*, can be produced at all. For in production the director and actors must choose one of the two alternatives: in performance Mrs. Smith will either be kissed or she will not be kissed. Performance in the flesh, in the concrete, does not allow for the act and the non-act simultaneously. To the degree that the playwright wishes to illustrate that contraries are identical, he is bound to fail; he mocks himself, and calls attention to the absurdity of trying to be truly absurd, by writing stage directions that can never be followed.

Yet the play is performed, and one thing or another happens. But *should* it have happened? And what is the true significance of what has happened, caught between should and should not?

It is in the indecisiveness at the heart of the play that we most often feel, face, and wrestle with ambiguity. If the playwright means to say that nothingness *is*, and that contraries are identical, he is not showing us that. If he means to say that we are behaving contrarily, and so seducing ourselves toward loss of identity, then that is another matter—but is he? The play hovers between two poles, seeming to embrace both and neither.

Sometimes we come from an Absurd play thoroughly enraged, perhaps because we suspect we have been flirting with nothingness that is meant to be genuine and is not, perhaps because we feel we have been victimized by untalented opportunists who have made the irrational features of the form an excuse for self-indulgence. And sometimes we come away somewhat pleased, having been touched by the enforced death of the grandmother in *The Sandbox* or by the grotesque arms stretched around a boxful of memories in *Krapp's Last Tape*, or having found ourselves unexpectedly moved to laughter by the butcher's ever-growing skyscraper (one entire floor devoted to "used meat") in Arnold Weinstein's *The Red Eye of Love*. In these cases, however, we are going on faith: we say to ourselves that *because* we responded in this way or that, the play itself must mean this or that. In one sense this is a good enough way to react to any art form (it is spontaneous, unprejudiced, uncluttered by excess baggage), though ideally one might wish to feel emotionally and intellectually satisfied at the same time. But in another sense such a response can be treacherous. For instance, I now do not know what I think of *Krapp's Last Tape* because I have discovered that the gesture that moved me most and seemed of greatest significance in performance—the stretching of those arms about the very memories Krapp had spent an hour reviling—seems to have been an invention of the director and does not appear in the published text.

Anyone who has listened to the laughter that greets so many avant-garde plays knows it is, for the most part, an insecure laughter. *Was* that last line or bit of business intended to be funny in its grotesquerie, or was it an open door to Hell as chilling as any Hieronymus Bosch ever designed? If I laugh, will I be advertising myself as a sophisticate, a man in the know, or as an uneasy boor? Nothing is commoner than an author's suggestion that what is happening on the stage bears some relation to the methods of the Marx Brothers or of old-fashioned burlesque comedians, just as there is a Spanish avant-garde play invitingly entitled *Buster Keaton's Walk*. The hopeful comparison is not new. Twenty-five years ago W. H. Auden and Christopher Isherwood wrote a stage direction for their *Ascent of F-6* asking that the principals "jump on each other's shoulders . . . and behave in general like the Marx Brothers." It was at this moment that the play fell apart. For the parallel is simply not acceptable. No thunderclap of laughter unifies the audience, instantly and unselfconsciously, as it does when Groucho is at his best, and for a very clear reason. The delights of the Marx Brothers' incongruity are only possible in a congruent world in which the elegant Margaret Dumont stands starched and indignant in defense of all the proprieties while Groucho behaves so improperly. The humor is in the irreverence for what is reasonable, the fingers snapped at a world essentially coherent and stable.

The Theatre of the Absurd, in its central ambiguity, is without such an anchor. There is no pattern of expectation in it from which a delinquent may depart. Instead of having one delightfully displaced person in collision with another who is clearly placed, we are confronted with simultaneous instabilities. Whatever they do to or with one another is merely arbitrary, as it is arbitrary in *The Caretaker* for three men to pass on, snatch away, and put down a suitcase a number of times in succession, or for a Fire Chief in *The Bald Soprano* to enter a living room in which he is neither expected nor unexpected in order to tell a joke that is not a joke.

Irrelevance is funny because it is irrelevant *to* something. Arbitrariness, lacking a defined point of departure, produces a mixed, timid, tentative response. If the author is razing the present world in order to rebuild, then his purpose is satirical and hilarity may be appropriate. If, on the other hand, his purpose is to deny substance altogether, which means in passing that he must deny the substance of comedy, then laughter can only be the frightened and hysterical response of an embarrassed child.

If it is difficult to respond openly, and with confidence, to the core of an Absurd play just now, it is because the playwright himself is not, at the core, being open. At the moment nearly every playwright of the school is keeping his own counsel as to the ultimate significance of his ultimate symbol, as to the precise intention of his philosophical thought. In the innermost recess of the play, there is not so much a bedrock of conviction as one more veil. The play may be saying "Stop this nonsense" or it may be saying "Stop, all is nonsense." For reasons of professional caution or of private uncertainty, in fear of being found out or in fear of misrepresenting the truth, the philosophical dramatist avoids committing himself to a defined philosophical position. He chooses not to make the choice at the heart; he makes the kernel itself ambiguous.

Thus he has in effect inverted the methods of those who have gone before him. Molière, the poet, keeps his character elusive at the surface; we watch Alceste behave now this way, now that, most contrarily. But the tension of his surface contrariness leads us to his identity. By the time he leaves us, we know that we know him; we know that the man moving away from us down the loneliest of roads, hurling imprecations over his shoulder as he abandons us forever, is a real man. The movement has been circuitous, but its course has been determined by a center. The anti-dramatist, philosophical precisionist that he is, restricts his terms at the surface as firmly as Beckett restricts his heroine to a home in the sand, or as Ionesco restricts his hero who does not become a rhinoceros (there is no choice here, the last man on earth yearns to become a rhinoceros and *cannot*). But as we mine the explicit surface to see where the mother lode is, we do not come closer to a subterranean reality; we become more and more aware that there may not be one. The philosopher has carved his road markers absolutely and then, in a coquettish gesture that may have been born of irresponsible prankishness and may have been born of real pain, refused to say what they mark the way to. There is, or is not, a reality at the end of the road.

Walter Kerr, drama critic of the New York Herald Tribune *and author of books as well as co-author of plays, contributes frequently to* HORIZON. *His most recent essay, "What Will the Robin Do Then, Poor Thing?" appeared in March, 1962.*

WHERE WILL THE BOOKS GO?

A scientist ponders the revolution that may soon be caused by microprinting;

Physicists these days are discussing a question that is going to be of interest to every literate person: How small a book can we make—and still read? Like many of the physicists' questions, this one may seem merely microscopic and clever, but it bears the seeds of immense social change.

Already, of course, we are in the early stages of the micro-book revolution. Business records, library copies of back issues of newspapers, thousands of Ph.D. dissertations, and many tens of thousands of "unpublished" and mimeographed research reports for government agencies are stored on film. This method gives a reduction of 40 to 60 times in the area of each page when it is photographed on standard 35-millimeter film. A second and higher degree of reduction is offered by microcards, which are coming into use in many libraries. On these, each page of a book is reduced in area by 500 to 1,000 times, so that the whole book can be printed on an ordinary-sized library catalogue card.

But why stop here? These reductions are still quite trivial compared to a third degree of reduction that we might get by going to the fundamental "optical limit." This is what is used in the "microdot" system, which has already been effective as an espionage device. In this scheme a page of print is shrunk photographically down to the smallest size at which the individual letters can still be read through a high-powered optical microscope. The reduction in size from ordinary printing is then about 500 to 1,000 times in height and width, so that each letter and each page and each drawing and photograph is reduced in area by as much as one million times.

This microscopic printing was the limit, I said? Yes, but only the optical limit. A fourth degree of reduction is now possible that can go as far beyond this as the hydrogen bomb goes beyond the atomic bomb.

Two years ago the theoretical physicist Richard P. Feynman of the California Institute of Technology gave a talk to the American Physical Society, which he called "There's Plenty of Room at the Bottom." He pointed out that organic life is able to store its genetic information right at the ultimate molecular level, "printing" it in the form of long "coded" chains of atoms in the chromosomes. Why shouldn't we also try to approach this level with our intellectual information, by storing our words and pages at least near the limit of magnification of the electron-microscope? This would not be quite down to the level of molecular structure, but it could easily be "ultramicroscopic," say 100 times smaller—and perhaps in a few years 1,000 times smaller—than the limit of the optical microscope.

To make this suggestion concrete, Feynman proposed that we could "write" or "print" on a thin metal film by "etching" it away with a fine controlled "pencil" of electrons. A pencil 50 to 100 angstroms in diameter could write letters 300 to 500 angstroms high—that is, about one or two millionths of an inch. In Germany, recently, the physicist G. Möllenstedt proved the method would work and published an electron-microscopic picture of his initials—"G. Mö."—which he wrote on a metal film with an electronic pencil 80 angstroms wide.

With a little further work along these lines we could easily reach an electron-microscope reduction by 100,000 times in each dimension, so that an ordinary page of print would shrink to about one micron by two microns in area. One square millimeter—the area of the head of a pin, which for years has been the cliché of comparison in all such discussions—could then hold 1,000 books of 500 pages each. An ordinary sheet of paper represents about 20,000 of these millimeter areas, so that it would then hold all of the 20 million or so different books that are supposed to be contained in all the world's libraries.

Actually we may never have to compress our knowledge to this extent, but the possibilities offered are tantalizing. Are we now printing too many books and magazines, newspapers and reports, and forms in quintuplicate for filing? Many people think so. Robert Graves has even suggested that to recover our sanity we should abolish all paper and forbid anyone to have writing materials except poets. (He is a poet.) But the example of the pinhead library shows that we could have been publishing ten or a hundred times as much as we have been and our total production would still fit inside, let us say, the head

By JOHN RADER PLATT

a library in every living room will be able to contain the entire written record of humanity

of a thumbtack. And we could go on writing and printing for a million generations and still not even take up the volume of a big shelf of books today.

Once you see that there is room for it all, you begin to wonder, indeed, if we should not publish much that we do not. In my universal library I want to have *everything. All* the letters in the attics, *all* the rejected manuscripts, *all* the "unpublished" reports, *all* the interoffice memos with ideas in them. Index them properly and cross-index them, so that we can find them when we want them—without wading through them when we do not!—and each may someday have its important little drop to contribute to the interrelated stream of human thought.

The ultramicrobooks I have described are probably unnecessarily extreme for the moment, but I believe that the simpler microbooks, at our third, optical-microscope level of reduction, are already a foreseeable development. I think it is interesting to note what becomes possible even at this level and how it may change our reading habits and attitudes. The conversion to microcopies is already coming fast because the sheer physical volume of full-sized "readable" books and documents is what makes them expensive to handle, to mail, or even to store on shelves for long periods. Any kind of microstorage cuts down on such costs, in library stacks as well as business files. The inconvenience of reading microcopies in a projection machine, or even the expense of making an occasional full-sized photographic copy, therefore becomes bearable for the masses of material not needed very often.

The trouble is that the advantages of microstorage are institutional, while its disadvantages are personal. We have come to enjoy the sensory pleasures we have associated for the past few hundred years with the life of the intellect—the pleasures of browsing among the shelves, of handling real books and smelling the print, of flipping through the pages to look at the pictures or the endings, or even (librarians, look away!) of turning down the page corners or writing vigorous rebuttals in the margins. Our big libraries have already made book-reading a formal chore, with their forbidding circulation desks and their elaborate call-card systems and long delays. Some of us may fear that if we now have to read microbooks only on projection screens, the literate pleasures will vanish completely. It may be research, but it is not *reading*.

Actually, of course, the libraries will continue to have space for about as many full-sized books as they ever had. What microcopies will do is permit libraries to add a great deal of rarer material to their collections—for those who are interested in seeing it even in microform—without having to expand the buildings. Can any library-lover object to that? What is needed may simply be some new inventions, some improvements in projectors and film-handling, so that microfilm could be projected on a well-lit, well-focused screen in front of a comfortable chair, with simple controls at hand for "selecting books" and "turning the pages." If such a "microbook-reader" were really pleasant and easy to use, every home would begin to want one and every library would want dozens, and we all might begin to prefer getting our books, and reading them, in the light, inexpensive microfilm form.

Already we have gone from picture hieroglyphs, and cuneiform writing with a stylus on clay and stone tablets, to writing with ink on papyrus rolls; then to vellum books about 2,000 years ago; to paper books about 1,200 years ago; to printing with movable type about 500 years ago; and in the last few decades to many diversified methods of printing—and photocopying. Is any one of these historical methods uniquely precious in the physical form it takes? Probably each has seemed so, to a generation brought up to respect it. I can imagine a time when the Minoan palace warehouses were bursting at the seams with baked clay records, but a dedicated record-keeper nonetheless would show a good deal of resistance to the new papyrus scrolls. With their long inscriptions written in streaks of fading ink paste on a thin rolled-up inflammable sheet, they must have seemed terribly complicated, impermanent, inaccessible, and expensive to a man accustomed to the simplicity and solidity of clay tablets.

We feel much the same way about microfilm today. But we

must remember that what is precious is not the physical "artifacts" of a system of writing but the "mentifacts," the human communications they contain. When our books change into new forms, children brought up to love the things of the mind will come to treat these forms with the same feelings of respect and familiarity and pleasure that we have had for the old ones.

And then we will have real microlibraries. At the optical-microscope level of reduction, all those 20 million books in all the world's libraries could be put on a desk top, or in a cabinet beside the record player. With an optical-microscope system permitting a reduction in area of about one million times, our 20 million volumes could be photocopied into 20 average volumes, about half the size of a standard encyclopedia. Each sheet in our hypothetical 20 volumes might contain, say, 2,000 books of 500 pages each; and each volume 500 such sheets, or one million books; with a total of 10,000 sheets in all the 20 volumes, about the number in an encyclopedia today.

What would such a dream library cost? Probably a few hundred dollars for the projection microscope, at medical-microscope or slide-projector prices. Probably a few hundred dollars for the 10,000 microprinted sheets, if they were "contact prints" made from master sheets, at costs comparable to present costs for contact photocopies. (The fine-grained film costs more, but mass production should bring it down.) Probably a few hundred dollars per user—if there were, say, 200,000 or more professional users—for copying all the 20 million books onto the master sheets, at present copying rates. Perhaps a thousand dollars or so for a special storage rack with a mechanical selector, allowing for the fact that such a mechanism must be delicate and precise, but also for the fact that there should be economies in mass production.

And certainly we should allow comparable sums, maybe a thousand dollars or two, for royalties and copyrights to permit recent and current books to be microprinted in these desk libraries. Add it all up and, if these "iffy" estimates are not too far off, the total cost per Universal Library might then be in the three to six thousand dollar range.

This could cost far less and be worth more, and would certainly have more buyers, than those desk-top electronic computers that have been talked about for years. The sum is not much more than many students and professional people pay for books and journals over, say, a twenty-year period, and is much less than the cost of a reading room or study in a new house, so that such a library system might be built into many houses and apartments, much as hi-fi systems are built in today. My guess is that there might be more than half a million doctors, lawyers, engineers, scientists, and teachers in the United States who might buy such a microlibrary on the installment plan at this price. After all, it would contain in one package all those expensive medical books, all the texts and back volumes of scientific journals, all the encyclopedias; and everything else, too. Plus all the library apparatus of catalogues, guides, and indexes to help find things in all the other books you would now own.

At this price, a desk-top library, or several of them, would be a "must" for newspaper offices, publishers, industrial companies with patent or reference problems, and every grammar school, high school, and public library. However many the initial number of users, they would grow over the years as the easy looking-up of answers of all kinds began to be taken for granted. To finance the initial costs, such a system might be developed in stages, starting with technical literature, where the first users might be willing to pay more and where royalty and copyright problems might be less serious; the cost of completing the humanities and historical sections might then be relatively small. From a national point of view, even, the value of having a complete Library of Congress within reach of every student and teacher and scientist might be comparable to the value of our great highway systems, and the initial development might be deserving of similar government support.

Where will the books go? Where *everybody* can read them—which is where they have always belonged.

At this point I must make a confession. I have spent this much space in speculating on these technical and commercial

aspects, not because I am so much interested in the details, which might be quite different from what I have imagined, but because the desk-top library is an especially graphic image to keep in mind in trying to get a real feeling for some of the problems connected with the scope and growth of human knowledge. It is equivalent to taking us up to a high place from which we can see it all. Just as when we first get a view of our whole city from a nearby hill or from a plane, we suddenly see the relations of the parts and the true size of man's intellectual achievements at a single glance—something we saw before only house by house and street by street.

It is only when you consider seriously the possibility of owning, of having at your fingertips, and being able to read in your own chair, all the world's literature and learning, that you can actually begin to think of this knowledge as a whole and see what our future attitude toward it may be like as we as a race grow more mature. The actual users of microlibraries, when they finally do come along, will grow up in the daily presence of this totality. They will be reminded continually of just what is before them, and of how complex it is; and as a result will begin to use it in a masterful way almost unimaginable for our present-day scholars, buried as they are in some corner of it, surrounded by their physical acres of library stacks.

Consider how your own reactions might change, step by step, if you were a scholar or layman in 1970 or 2070, as you begin to get used to having at hand, all the time, anything you want to know that human beings know. When you get your first Universal Library, very likely you will hurry to dip into it here and there—to find all the entrancing and unavailable books you have not read before. Probably for a while you will also be fascinated in looking at all the subjects—microbrowsing—on any sheet you open to, and reading samples of the ones that look interesting or have interesting pictures. This is the way a bright twelve-year-old acts when his family gets its first adult encyclopedia, and it is not a bad way of exploring and getting the feel of how to use the system. But after a few days you will come to realize, as he does, that at almost every point

the material is too hard or too trivial or not really interesting, and that certainly there is too much of it. And you will begin to use the Library more and more selectively and purposefully, to read specific things only when you are referred to them or when a question comes up or when your interest is aroused.

At about this point, with the microlibrary, you will also begin to realize something new; namely, how fast additional human discourse is coming in. The 300,000 or so new titles per year that the Library of Congress now adds to its stacks will double our 20 Universal Volumes in a generation or so. And they do not even include all the material published under old titles—the magazines and newspapers and the 300,000 new scientific articles per year, with 600 per day of medical articles alone. All this adds up to a new Addition Sheet with the contents of 2,000 ordinary-sized books every day or two. Not much in terms of the pinhead library we talked about earlier, but staggering in individual terms. When the Addition Sheets begin to arrive regularly in the mail, you will be continually reminded not only that you cannot read everything ever written but that you cannot even keep up with one-thousandth part of the new material being added every day. And this is as true for the scientist or philosopher or scholar as it is for the layman.

We begin, then, to wonder seriously: How much can an intelligent man know, and how much should he try to know, of previous or current human learning?

From our present vantage point we see that the number of books a man can digest in a lifetime is very small. A vigorous editor or book critic may scan four books in a day, or perhaps 1,000 a year. But to read and digest articles or books worth reading, the rate is much lower, and the average literate adult probably cannot absorb more than two to four books per week, even including those in his own specialty. If we say 160 books per year for 50 years, or 8,000 books, we will be describing a very bookish lifetime.

What it adds up to is four of the microprinted sheets out of the 10,000 in our Universal Library.

We realize suddenly that even the men most famous in his-

"In my universal library I want everything."

tory for their learning could not have known from their own reading more than a microscopic fraction of the lore of their times. The supposition that there was a time when a man could "know everything" is one of those Great Man myths that worshipers use to make their contemporaries seem small and themselves seem excusable. Most of us today are omnivorous readers—or scanners—of newspapers, magazines, current books, and even encyclopedias. We were brought up reading. We were brought up to think it is good, and it is. I suspect that millions of us read more than any of the great men of the past. But do we profit more from it?

The trouble is that we were not brought up selecting. This is the wisdom of the wise men, not that they knew but that they chose. It is a wisdom anyone can practice. We are harassed and hypnotized by print. But it is time to stop being passive about how we spend our minds. Are you not frightened by the thought of that long path of newsprint unrolling ahead of you down the years? Put some other kind of print beside your coffee cup. After you have read some of the newspaper, like an intelligent citizen, read something that touches your real interests more closely, like an intelligent human being.

There is no need to be all grim and serious about this, of course. We all have different jobs to do, and different intellectual hungers, and we all need different kinds of things to read at different times, from whodunits to history, from *Pogo* to the *Perennial Philosophy*. Often nothing will restore our sanity like gales of laughter. Nevertheless it is salutary to ask yourself when you next reach for a book, is this one of the 8,000—or the 4,000 or the 2,000—I really want to build into my life? It clarifies your choices wonderfully.

And why not 4,000 or 2,000? Since the most a man can read is trivial anyway in comparison with the total human library, why not enrich yourself by spending more time and thought on just the 40 per year or the 20 per year that are most relevant to your own condition and purposes? The original references, not the texts. (You could think, in between.) The original authors, not the critical reviews. (You could live, in between.)

The original poets, not the discussions of poetry. (You could write, in between.)

All this is a considerable oversimplification, of course. How does a man know what he would profit most from when choosing his reading? He must get advice and read reviews and decide whose judgment he trusts. How does he know where to find it? By looking it up in the indexing systems and hoping they are accurate and complete. How does he know what his own interests really are? Ah, there's the problem. By self-exploration, in the light of the challenges he gets from being interested in what he reads. It is all a cumulative problem, with another step in self-development after every round. But we see that evaluation, selection, indexing, are all intertwined; and the user of the desk-top library will be reminded of that every day.

The indexing problem is of the greatest concern today, especially with the flood of new material and the masses of microfilmed documents, most of them hard to classify by the old categories. Many librarians and scientists and government agencies are trying to invent more satisfactory indexing systems that will keep all these bits of information from getting lost through inadequate indexing or cross-indexing. It all makes me think we may be approaching a time when scholars and scientists will find it convenient to memorize the index numbers of their own interests, and to arrange that only the papers and documents will be sent to them whose index numbers coincide with theirs. "I'm 437 and 411.293. What are you?" Today the doctor can flip through his medical journal when it arrives in the mail, stopping at a familiar name or subject or at a figure that interests him. How long before he can scan as quickly and rewardingly a microfilm strip of the same journal, or of all the medical journals? Just as long as it takes for us to begin indexing and cross-indexing articles in advance, so that he can turn instantly to what interests him.

But even if this problem could be solved, we would still have to evaluate. The outsider cannot know what is important and what is trivial or wrong in the books of category 411.293, except by getting the evaluations of one or two insiders; and

"A universal man is one who refuses to be overwhelmed."

DAVID LEVINE

he will still have to decide for himself whether their judgment is reliable. Every time we use other men's knowledge, we face this question, whether we are conscious of it or not. Can we doubt that even the young Socrates was confronted by it when he acquired, from his teachers or from his own experience and judgment, his ideas of what problems *not* to be interested in and what books *not* to read?

A man who has well-educated himself knows how the different parts of the body of knowledge fit together, even though he cannot know all the details except in one or two tiny corners. He knows which parts are generally relevant to his interests. He decides for himself when to read the Gee-Whiz reporters or the digesters and when to leave their tidbits untouched. He knows what he wants to explore more carefully or contribute to, and what he does not. But even in areas outside his own competence, where he must to some degree trust the experts and evaluators—as Socrates and Aristotle and every other philosopher or synthesizer has had to trust them—he can still tell sloppy reasoning from sound, and to some degree judge these various experts for himself.

Those universal men who were supposed to know something about every science are not really celebrated for the completeness of their information but for this kind of selection and comparison, judgment and insight. Their learning was microscopic, compared to all human learning, as it always will be; their judgment was large, as it always can be.

The reason we do not have such men in our time is that we lack confidence in our choice and judgment. As scholars and scientists and philosophers and teachers, we get started in one specialty and often go on all our lives without ever looking around. We feel surrounded and small, and we may talk about being overwhelmed by the sweep and complexity of modern knowledge. I have often heard scientists say, "There is just too much!" But we need not feel this way any more than the scholars of old; what one man can know is not significantly smaller now than it was then, compared to the vast unknown total. As soon as we begin to put facts in their place and to reason about larger relationships, we can begin to recover the universal attitude. A universal man is simply a man who refuses to be overwhelmed.

I think that if we ever come to have widespread microlibraries, adequately indexed, with the whole world of learning and letters immediately at hand, the universal attitude will also become widespread. Without it, in fact, no one will be able to employ a universal microlibrary effectively. Some people will use the library to read for pleasure—almost everyone, let us hope. Some will use it to look up scholarly or technical or managerial answers. Some, to find points of departure for their own new contributions to knowledge. But I think all of these users will acquire an air of intellectual comprehension and assurance, like a man with a brain who knows what he is about.

For the microlibrary will begin to have some of the coherent qualities of a brain. If all our knowledge can be brought together in a familiar system within everyone's reach, the increase in the intelligence and effectiveness of our behavior should be astonishing. The world's knowledge, kept up to date, will become a closer and closer adjunct to all kinds of decision-making and action. The microscopic library, with its interrelated information instantly accessible, will make possible a new awareness of relations and consequences, a widespread and rapid interplay of human ideas and inventions, and a directness of collective decision such as we could not have imagined without it. Because it is small and closely knit, delays and uncertainties are reduced as they are in a real brain. In our use of it we can therefore begin to approach the unity and directness of our own complex biological decision-making and memory system, with its similarly interrelated and microscopic neuron elements, similarly packed in a compact space, within a single skull. Microlibraries would be a memory and the beginnings of a universal brain for the whole human race.

John Rader Platt has recently published The Excitement of Science, *in which one of his contributions to* HORIZON *will be found. He is a professor of physics at the University of Chicago.*

A photographer's portfolio documents his love for an enduring people in their timeless land

The New-Zealand-born photographer Brian Brake has traveled extensively—to Fiji, Russia, Nigeria, Israel, and India as well as North America—besides visiting Communist China, when the pictures in the next eight pages were made. He provides the note that follows on his feeling for that eminently paintable and photogenic place.

China is not a country where one arrives. To be there at all is sufficient, for—once you are there—the rest of the world does not exist. China is a pattern; there the pattern belongs to its country more intimately than in any other land I know. I have seen the laced water of the paddy fields in many places in the East; but in China, perhaps because of the trees, or because of the flat silk look of it, the impression it makes is manifestly Chinese.

What is it, this ingrained Chinese-ness? Perhaps it is the way that the long civilization and the astronomical millions of people have profoundly modified their country. Three or four thousand years of intensive, detailed gardening—that is what I feel they have done throughout China. Slowly they have made the land their own. Now it is special to them, like their faces, their language, their painting, their boats, and even their toys.

This quality seems to have passed down through Chinese time without radical alteration, absorbing and redefining everything that comes from without. Even now, under a system as alien as that of the Mongols in the Yuan dynasty, it is the undivided Chinese-ness of the manner of thought that strikes a visitor like myself. On the following pages you will find some of my photographs of China. I hope they express, more tangibly than my words, something of the beauty of China that is, and always will remain, uniquely its own.

BRIAN BRAKE

China of the Chinese

FIRST PAGE: *With literacy comes public print. This man with the escaping shirttail has stopped to read a notice posted by the Lanchow Locomotive Athletic Association Information Section. "The basketball team of the National Locomotive Workers will shortly be coming to Lanchow . . ." the legend reads. "It is hoped that our staff and workers will turn out to see the games in force."*

SECOND PAGE: *The theory that nature imitates art is again and again confirmed by the Chinese landscape, which mirrors painting as faithfully as these junks, ferrying cargo, are reflected in the waters of Kunming Lake, near Kunming, in Yunnan province.*

THIRD PAGE: *Toy birds of paper and feathers, for sale by the wayside in Lanchow, display the Chinese capacity for making the most of meager materials. The tails revolve when the birds are pulled through the air, like kites, at the end of a length of string.*

FOURTH AND FIFTH PAGE: *It is early morning in a newly planted rice paddy near Chengtu, in Szechwan. Each field is separated from the next by banks of earth, and along one of them a peasant pushes a wheelbarrow. The trees at right in the distance are bamboo, the giant grass whose spiky leaf pattern has for so many centuries delighted the Chinese eye.*

SIXTH PAGE: *The force of the past is especially felt in the Chinese drama, where a popular tradition has sucessfully been based on a near-*

perfect stylization of technique. In his dressing room in a Peking theatre, Li Shao Ch'uan, the most famous of all the artists who play the Monkey King, makes up for that role in Journey to the West, *one of the traditional works performed by the Peking Opera.*

SEVENTH PAGE: *From all over China a convention of leading Buddhist monks has gathered in Sian, an ancient Chinese capital on a tributary of the Yellow River. Here, under the flags of the Communist regime, they have assembled in a courtyard of the Temple of the Reclining Dragon to be photographed. The four monks in the center of the front row are of the highest rank in China. The film case of the photographer, who is using a far-from-modern panoramic camera, identifies him as coming from the "Photographic Department of the Municipal Services of Sian City."*

EIGHTH PAGE: *In at least one respect the "new" China defers to the old. Many Chinese, who previously had little idea of the wealth of their culture, can now examine the exhibits in the huge new National Museum in Peking, founded in 1959 to mark the 10th Anniversary of the Communist Revolution. These dragon-entwined columns support a modern copy of an armillary sphere, the original dating from the Sung Dynasty. It was used to calculate the Chinese calendar and is known, in Chinese, as the* Hun Yi, *or* Hun T'ien Yi—the *"all-about-the-heavens instrument."*

ARCHITECT'S HERO: LOUIS KAHN

In his angular forms and ardent theories a profession

searching for prophets has found its newest vision

With good reason, people seldom look twice at the random piles of brick, steel, and concrete that stand along our streets. A rare and curious exception is the angular, startling structure erected at Philadelphia in 1958–60, the Richards Medical Research Building at the University of Pennsylvania (see illustrations on pages 58, 62, and 63). Its architect is Louis I. Kahn, a Philadelphian, who serves that university as its senior professor of architecture. No more than a few of his adventurous designs have actually been built and, though they are highly regarded by architects, he is known only slightly outside his profession. But Kahn has arrived on the scene at a time when architecture is hungry for daring new departures. It has come near the end of the paths laid down by Frank Lloyd Wright, Mies van der Rohe, and Le Corbusier; and among the architects now practicing only Louis Kahn seems capable of rising to their stature. In a profession that dotes on heroes, he is one of the few heroes America has.

By conventional standards the Richards Medical Building is not a beautiful one. You are likely not to like it when you see it. Its brick towers, massive and stark, bristle on the skyline; the concrete structure below seems brutish: ugly pipes, ducts, and wires gnarl its ceilings; the concrete columns and walls throughout bear the corrugations left like birthmarks by the wooden molds. If you seek a quiet, serene, or pretty architecture you will not find it here.

The man who made this uncommon structure—and, before it, Yale University's remarkable new Art Gallery (page 61)—is himself an uncommon man. Kahn was born on the Estonian island of Sarema in 1901. Short and sparse, he moves nervously, talking of light, or space, or order. As he tells how light will strike a wall, his hands work to simulate the brick and sun that his high, hoarse voice describes.

Kahn's office is a modest loft where men work, not nine to five, but—tieless and in shirt sleeves—at any hour, day or night. When I saw him recently, his young staff, drawn to him from many countries, occupied the second floor of a block of stores near the center of Philadelphia. I climbed the dark stairs (there was no elevator) and entered a wide place in a corridor set off by cheap, rough partitions and furnished with old wooden chairs.

When two men left the inner office, a secretary waved me into Kahn's room. Darkness had come upon it, and only the warm afternoon light, reflected from the building across the street, entered the large window directly ahead. Seated at his desk alongside the window, Kahn was a silhouette, holding the telephone to his ear. Without breaking his conversation, he threw out his hand to me; it did not shake mine but literally pulled me down into the seat opposite him.

He was having trouble ending his conversation. "I ought not to do it," he said. "That's good of you, very good, but look, I can't." On the sill was a pile of books and papers; a bowl contained an orange and some wrinkled apples, a Cézanne still life

57

By ALBERT BUSH-BROWN

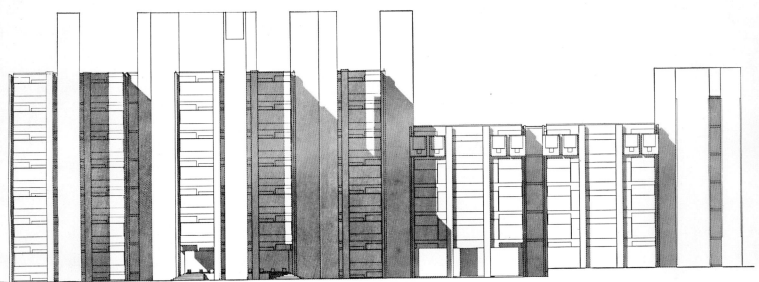

left uneaten. Books, maps, sketches, and photographs were scattered about as though in a student's study. There was the look of a place where men fought for ideas. Across the stained, board floor, a large model of a building leaned against the wall; above, drooping from a single thumbtack, hung a colossal photostat of Robert Adam's Roman phantasy, an eighteenth-century city of pantheons, baths, fora, temples, basilicas, colosseums, and libraries. Otherwise, there was only a table—a mere door resting on a trestle—some rocks, a brick, a shell, and a branch. "Thanks, thanks, maybe later, yeah, not now though, O.K.? Right, right," and Kahn returned the telephone to its cradle, as though he had won a moral battle.

Such temptations to disperse his talent have come to Louis Kahn only recently. After he was graduated from the School of Architecture at the University of Pennsylvania in 1924, he served as draftsman in various offices in Philadelphia, beginning with the city architect, with whom he worked on Philadelphia's Sesqui-Centennial Exhibition in 1925–26. He had trained under Paul Cret, the brilliant French critic at Penn who designed one of America's finest Beaux-Arts buildings, the Pan-American Union at Washington; thus Kahn learned early the discipline of organizing spaces on a monumental public scale.

That training bore fruit in Kahn's association with George Howe, the remarkable Philadelphia architect and educator who (with William Lescaze) had produced the Philadelphia Saving Fund Society tower,

still one of the freshest of modern buildings. Together, Kahn and Howe designed defense housing, notably houses and apartments in Middletown, Pennsylvania. Then, with Oscar Stonorov, Kahn designed a neighborhood for Willow Run, the model community near the bomber plant northeast of Ypsilanti, Michigan, and Carver Court, a community for one hundred Negro war workers and their families at Coatesville, Pennsylvania. While those communities stand among the few good examples of war housing, they did not suggest any bold departures.

Where we can gauge Kahn's work before 1950, he seems to have been modest and conscientious but in no sense a pioneer. Only during his year in Europe, in 1950–51, as resident architect at the American Academy in Rome, did Kahn begin to grow into his own intensely personal comprehensive view of architecture. Sketchbook in hand, he traveled in Italy, making eloquent drawings of the Italian hill towns, capturing their masses by strokes of shadow. It was a critical experience for him, one that helped him see how architecture's true concern is the magnificent play of geometric form in light.

By 1946 Kahn was at Yale, teaching in the School of Architecture directed by his former associate George Howe. He and his students would work in the studio until it was closed at midnight, only to carry their conversation down the street to an all-night coffee shop. The ideas that mainly preoccupied them were three: first, how to achieve total co-ordination of a building, so that its

fine spaces, the light that reveals them, the structure that admits the light, and the mechanical equipment that moves fluids and gases through the building, all would be harmonized and made evident in the building's design; second, how to prevent obsolescence, how to make a building serve new occupants or permit rearrangements of space so that it could endure, usefully, for generations; and third, how to achieve a relationship among these spaces, so that the most important one—a sanctuary, a memorial, a library's reading room, or simply a place that is good for teaching—would stand forth, a master space, dominating the smaller spaces that serve it.

All these concerns had guided Kahn's design for the Yale Art Gallery and Design Center. To reconcile them, he turned his building's blank-walled side toward the street, opening its rear glass wall on the stairs and walls of an existing courtyard. Next, aided by a suggestion from the ever-inventive Buckminster Fuller, and with the help of Henry Pfisterer, Yale's professor of structural engineering, Kahn developed a deep ceiling of hollow triangles made of reinforced concrete (see opposite). Through the hollows run the ducts and pipes and wires, making both a display of their functions and a fascinating pattern. Light, demountable partitions stretching from floor to ceiling provide walls where and when they are required, giving the Gallery flexible interior arrangements.

To Kahn's credit, shortcomings in his buildings plague him. What worries him about the Yale Gallery is that the detach-

Kahn's most celebrated achievement is the Richards Medical Building in Philadelphia, shown opposite as it will look with an added wing, in a sketch that emphasizes his love of light and shadow, and his decision to build here, not a boxlike structure, but a wall of connected towers. At right Kahn stands beneath the recessed ceiling of the Yale Art Gallery (1953), in New Haven, the first of his designs (as one critic wrote) "that made architects sit up and take notice."

able panels are far from soundproof; he wonders now whether the need for changes in floor plan are best served by erecting temporary partitions like those at Yale or by having a series of generalized, separate rooms; and he regrets not having any permanent, large spaces modeled by natural light. In 1957 he was still challenging himself with these problems as he commuted between Yale, where he was chief critic in the Master's Program for Architecture, and Philadelphia, where Holmes Perkins, the new Dean of Architecture at the University of Pennsylvania, had appointed him professor.

Sometimes difficult issues become easier to clarify when encountered on a small scale with few complications. So it was with Kahn's opportunity to design a bathhouse for a recreation center at Trenton, New Jersey. Only locker spaces and dressing rooms were required. Not having to contend with machinery, many functions, or difficult structure, Kahn clustered four simple pavilions around an open central court (see page 60). The result is one of the cleanest and most immediately intelligible of his designs.

Kahn's way of speaking often seems to be an unequal struggle between his meaning and his words. "To begin is the time of belief in form," he has said. "Design is the maker that serves this belief." What he himself believes is better served by what he builds, and surely the nearest he has come to realizing that belief is the Richards Building; it is Kahn's through and through. He deplored the dreary, noxious cells that

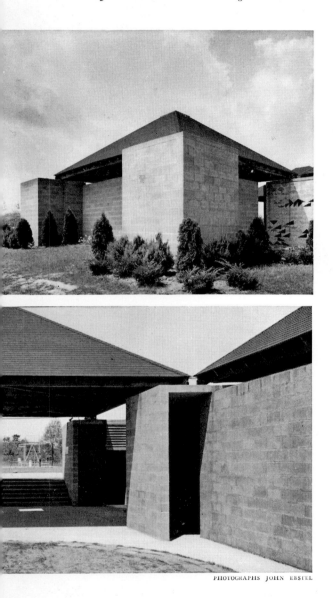

PHOTOGRAPHS JOHN EBSTEL

*Opposite: The Yale Art Gallery turns an
elegant but blank brick wall toward the
street (above), thus adapting itself
to the Romanesque dignity of the former
Gallery at right. On its other side,
however, the Gallery is all glass, opening
out onto a campus courtyard, providing
the students with north light, and revealing
itself (at night, below) to be filled with
paintings, sculpture, and the patterns of its
movable partitions and honeycomb ceiling.*

line the corridors of most modern laboratories, where foul air and gloomy rooms provide a setting self-evidently incompatible with scientific study. He argued that the best design for research is a series of studios served by clean air and natural light. The Richards Building would have to stand on the north side of a botanical garden, joining two older buildings to the east and west, with a pedestrian walk on the campus north of the site. An isolated, self-contained, classical sort of structure would only intrude on an already confused and crowded site. Therefore Kahn decided to build a wall, not a building but a series of connected towers.

He arranged his studios in the towers so that each got as much natural light as possible, and then joined the towers together so as to form a rhythmical chain of pavilions. The Richards Building is a spectacular new example of this composition, not a single, self-enclosed form but a linked series of accented units: an architecture of rhythm rather than balance, of transition rather than termination, of open rather than closed form.

The Richards entrance lobby states its organizing principle. One single space, forty-seven feet square, the lobby is framed by pairs of H-shaped columns, rising to support the open trusses that carry each floor. They are made of concrete precast around steel rods stressed to high tension, giving them their sharp, knifelike profiles and smooth surfaces. They were swung onto each floor by a large crane that dropped them into place, and then drawn together by stretching the rods inside them, much as a sectional toy is brought erect by tightening its strings. The result is a crisp, unified geometry that both looks well and defines the building's interior spaces.

As we move about the structure we are offered powerful vistas from one tower across a small court and into the adjacent tower—spaces we can visualize as inside, then outside, then inside again. No previous architecture, in my opinion, is so powerfully three-dimensional in its ability to impress on you continuously, as you move through it, its functional, structural, and mechanical origins. The Richards Building can delight the visitor in the precise fit of trusses, the careful terminations of columns, the blunt vocabulary of its materials, colors, and textures. Above all, the monumental entrance under the protruding angle of

the tower, where the heavy beams overhead proclaim the weight they bear, is an achievement of form as compelling, urgent, and ascetic as the towers themselves.

The Richards Building won Kahn the Brunner Prize for 1960, annually awarded by the National Institute of Arts and Letters to the architect who contributes to "architecture as art." America's three professional journals rushed to applaud the center; New York's Museum of Modern Art devoted an entire exhibit to it. It was greeted enthusiastically in the architectural magazines of Japan, England, Italy, France, Germany, Scandinavia, South America, and Canada. Indeed, few recent buildings anywhere have been so well-celebrated.

Unfortunately, so much praise has had the effect of protecting the Richards Building from the criticism a great structure deserves. Kahn has become a hero too quickly, and too few of his fellow architects have listened to the scientists who have to work in his building. The latter complain that Kahn's rigorous integration of space, structure, and services has been purchased at too great an expense. The generalized studio spaces do not divide easily. Essential equipment—like refrigerators, public telephones, centrifuges, and cabinets—protrudes into the maze of corridors because no place was specially fitted to receive it. Secretaries have to sit in hallways. To correct glare, especially at the corners, the occupants have stretched aluminum foil across the windows, an unsightly improvisation that could have been avoided by protecting the windows and eliminating the transom.

Kahn admits some of these defects. The plans he has drawn for the United States Consulate in Luanda, Angola, show his search for an architecture that will deal with the sun, rain, and wind in southern Africa. A double roof, the upper layer intended to deflect the sun, the lower to catch rain water, will enable breezes to ventilate the space between. He proposes to counteract glare by shielding each window with a wall with an open slot in it, providing subdued light and a view, not from a dark interior to a brilliant outdoors, but first to intermediate intensity and only then to full sunlight.

A further development appears in his design for the First Unitarian Church in Rochester, New York. One majestic space, the central meeting hall, will be bathed in

The clean structural precision of the Richards Medical Building is shown in the model (below) of one of its towers. Floors are held in place by supporting columns between three tall brick stacks (two remove stale air, the slotted stack contains stairs). The cantilevered corners are cut away as the load decreases, making room for overhead windows. The dramatic force of Kahn's design is most fully felt in the entrance lobby (opposite), where form and functions meet in a severe and powerful symmetry.

light falling in four wells at the corners of the room—a strongly centralized form. The church will have a central, tall space surrounded by a corridor that serves smaller rooms—a spatial order Kahn favors. That organization, combined with the serrated profile, seems to be a sculptural form for which, contrary to his proclaimed theory, Kahn then finds a function. "The idea," Kahn has admitted openly about the Unitarian Church, "is to develop really quite frankly a silhouette."

One hopes Kahn's pursuit of the bold silhouette will not lead him astray. So many mature architects have been tempted, as Frank Lloyd Wright was tempted in his later days, to invent dazzlingly photogenic shells, often achieving sculptural effects by neglecting the functions they were meant to serve. This tends to be the weakness of any great building, including Kahn's, but now he has a fresh opportunity to escape from it and give his philosophy of form and function full expression. The opportunity is offered by the Salk Institute for Biology at Torrey Pines, on a cliff overlooking the Pacific near San Diego.

The assignment came to him unexpectedly. Jonas Salk heard Kahn speak to a medical group at Pittsburgh and then visited him in Philadelphia, where he saw the Richards Building and decided it was what his new research center needed. Kahn would not let him rest there. He drew and he talked, not only about research, but also about scientists and their ways of living. His proposal was, in effect, an academic village consisting of a residential community, laboratories and studies, and a meeting house, all connected by arcades, tree-shaded walks, gardens, and a cloister for meditation, poised on the cliff. The laboratories and studies appear to be an enormous improvement over those in the Richards Building, in fact in any building.

His plans for the Salk Center, a large scholarly community, bring Kahn closer to his greatest ambition, to design a city so wonderful that people will quit the suburbs in order to live in it. His would be a city fashioned like a forum, reminiscent of the one in the Robert Adam engraving that hangs in Kahn's office. In 1958 he hoped to have the opportunity in Philadelphia, where Mayors Joseph Sill Clark, Jr. and Richardson Dilworth had made city planning a rallying point for political reform. But the urge for reform became diverted into slum clear-

ance projects, isolating historic landmarks, building apartments at the urban fringes, and creating meretricious plazas framed by maudlin buildings, as at the modern Penn Center, where the automobile won out over the pedestrian.

Kahn was impatient of all this. He made his own plan. He gave different kinds of transportation separate avenues. Fast automobile traffic moved along expressways running around a large rectangle stretched from the Schuylkill to the Delaware and from Vine to Lombard Streets. The principal shopping street, Chestnut, would become a tree-lined pedestrian way with only trolley cars and local buses, while Walnut Street would be closed to motor traffic completely, linking Washington Square at the east with Rittenhouse Square at the west. Northward, one could walk through parks to a civic center at Logan Circle, and the present Penn Center (as it is now, isolated) would be extended from 18th Street westward to the river. The resulting shopping-business strip, three miles long, would be served by neighborhoods of row houses, while large towers within the city would be set aside for garages, with plazas at their centers. It was a visionary proposal, yet one of the most realistic so far devised for interweaving people, institutions, services, and vehicles into a forum where all could enjoy the amenities only a city can provide.

Unhappily, it played no part in the rebuilding of Philadelphia. Kahn is demonstrably one of the few great artists on the architectural scene in America. Yet his own city has withheld its greatest opportunity from him. That it did so is a tragic comment on a nation that so often remains indifferent to its artists, then suddenly discovers them, burdens them unmercifully, refrains from the criticism that will help them most, demands ever more original and novel things from them, disdains to use them at the critical moment for great civic tasks, then drops them with alacrity once their capacity for innovation—as it inevitably must—falters. To allow this to happen to Louis Kahn—as it has to other architects who were indulged in their sculptural dexterity but denied the chance to solve the urgent problems of our time—would be a loss we can ill afford.

Albert Bush-Brown, coauthor of The Architecture of America, *is president of the Rhode Island School of Design.*

CERVIN ROBINSON; OPPOSITE: GEORGE BARROWS—MUSEUM OF MODERN ART, N. Y.

In Print: EDWARD ADLER

The antithesis between Edward Adler and his art could not be more extreme. He is a gentle, frequently comical man, now nearing forty-two, of middle height, with blue eyes, thinning hair, and a thickening waist he pats now and then in absent reproach. He lives on 11th Street near Avenue D on New York's East Side, in a brick building well over a hundred years old; not a historical site, simply a slum. He is poor and drives a taxicab in order to support his family—a wife and two children to whom he is obviously deeply attached—and yet keep at the dedicated craft he has chosen for himself. For Edward Adler is the author of an astounding novel, *Notes From a Dark Street*, published earlier this year; and, as a novelist, he is regarded at the garage where he reports for work as a man apart—but no more so than the bookie who drifts in at night to take hackies' horse bets.

Adler looks, for the most part, like a run-down Talmudist, an impression he can exaggerate to heights of absurdity. For example, he has been known to improvise a living-room travesty on Robert Frost, T. S. Eliot, William Carlos Williams, and some other, more wispy poets. Adler, as Frost, is found seated on a compost heap in the baggage room of Grand Central Terminal. He is on his way, he explains, to Washington to give Congress a piece of his plain, wholesome mind. He is smoking a corn-silk cigarette, which he waves cheerfully at his passing peers, haranguing them sardonically in a cracked, high-pitched, singsong tone, his comments plentifully sprinkled with Yiddish. "*Genug*," he cries at Eliot. "Enough, Tom, with the *goyishen* metrics. English—write English." Shifting his bottom, he dips his arm into the heap. "*Nah!*" he invites Eliot, "have a handful."

Adler was born in the Gravesend Bay section of Brooklyn above his father's store, the kind of grocery shop New York Jews call an "appetizing," and he is to a large extent self-educated. After a mere six months at Brooklyn College, he entered the Army during World War II, served as a first lieutenant in the Troop Carrier Command, and was wounded in Europe. It was only in the Army that he began to read voraciously and attentively. He was stunned by Conrad's *Victory*; and it was then, years before he began to write, that he dimly perceived the possibilities of an artistic creed of pessimism, however it appeared to negate the undeniably fruitful manner in which he conducts his life.

Late in the forties, after knocking around in one odd job and another—as a bookmaker's runner in Florida, he submitted to a prearranged arrest—Adler started to write. *Notes From a Dark Street* underwent several metamorphoses in the half-dozen years it took to be written. Steadily, Adler stripped it of its simple naturalism and endowed it with the structure of a myth. He had read Dante and Joyce and he constructed the metaphor of the novel on the *Inferno*; the work became what Adler thinks of as his "joy at finding parallel myths all about me," expressed in parody, pun and paraphrase, hidden allusion, burlesque, and so on. Thus, all of the categories of sin defined by Dante are present; Part Two of the novel actually consists of thirty-four cantos, each representing a corresponding one in the *Inferno*, and begins halfway through the narrative for the reason that Dante began the *Divine Comedy* at the mid-point of his life. Adler even contrived—a contrivance organic enough to be undetectable save through exegesis—to pay tribute to Dante and Joyce, at the same time punning on their histories and, through the medium of his own purposefully degraded story, reflecting the degradation of his own century.

In *Notes From a Dark Street* the materials of common contemporary existence on the Lower East Side have been ordered and transmuted into a terrible cosmography far transcending its naturalistic events. The novel's aesthetic is as consciously propounded as, and not dissimilar to, those of a Nathanael West or a Flaubert. It is a hopeless but imperative involvement in the face of life's debasement and ultimate dissolution. Or, as one of the characters says explicitly, "The City is full of a hidden death which forces a stand on the issue of living." The book was less than a commercial success, but a measure of the force generated by it was an entire spectrum of critical reaction, ranging from "the literary find of the year" to an uneasy "sordid." It has since attracted a growing number of admiring readers who see in its author a major new talent, and in the novel a metaphor utterly appropriate to the times.

Adler is now at work on a second novel. This will carry forward, in other characters and with other metaphors, his thesis of the dying city-society. Just as Balzac saw himself as the secretary of French society, so Adler—in all modesty—wants to be the secretary of his own. "What I am trying to do," he said not long ago, "is the same thing, allegorically." He is aware of the apparent conflict between the melancholy of his work and the contentment—optimism, even—of his personal life, and he tried in an earlier draft of his novel to explain this paradox. He excised the passage, however, from his final script. "Were all the sky parchment," it reads, "and all our waters ink; were all of nature's reeds turned into writing implements, and I had eternity to record my understanding, I would record nothing if I did not understand that I was born for social and gregarious fullness, with wife and children and work genuinely of this real world; to earn my portion of peace and to cast a significance upon my existence which was otherwise starved and trivial."   GILBERT MILLSTEIN

Photograph by SAM FALK

On Stage: JOAN BAEZ

During the past two decades folk music in America has summoned up an audience of several million supporters, most but by no means all of them young people. The folk song is a singularly concise and accessible dramatic form: it sets a situation, tells a story, and portrays characters without leading the spectator through any intellectual mazes. Its melody line is readily absorbed, and it provides comfortable common ground for a great variety of listeners. Some singers, such as Pete Seeger, a popular wandering minstrel, invite their audiences to join in. Others sing and the audience listens, but not passively. Such a one is Joan Baez, a dark-haired, retiring, twenty-two-year-old girl whose voice—which is untrained—has been called by Robert Shelton of the New York *Times* "as lustrous and rich as old gold . . . unwinding like a spool of satin."

Miss Baez was introduced to her first large gathering of aficionados by Chicago's ebullient troubadour Bob Gibson, at the 1959 Newport Folk Festival, and the audience, which had come to see the famous Oscar Brand, Odetta, Earl Scruggs, and Jean Ritchie, could not have cared less. But when Miss Baez began her first verse in a clean, unaffected soprano, people sat up and looked at one another. How was her last name pronounced again? (By-ez.) Where had she been up to now? By the time she had concluded two duets with Gibson the spectators were congratulating themselves on having been present at the debut of a "star" among folk singers. Since that appearance she has recorded several albums and given concerts all over the country, ending a nationwide tour at Carnegie Hall in New York. (The performance was sold out two months in advance, with the audience finally crowding around the edges of the auditorium and stage.)

Of Irish-Mexican descent, Miss Baez was brought up in New York, Palo Alto, Boston, Baghdad—wherever her father, a nuclear physicist now working in Paris for UNESCO, happened to be employed. In 1958 he was teaching at Harvard, and Joan entered Boston University as a student at the Fine Arts School of Drama. She was eighteen and her qualifications consisted of one folk song, several guitar chords, and an instinctive appreciation of "good" rock 'n' roll music—the kind that is legitimately descended from the blues. But, discovering her voice, and intensively studying her guitar, she sang nightly at *espresso* coffee shops in the Boston area, where her name became as much a part of everyday conversation as Jack Kennedy's.

In an era when a deliberately cultivated "personality" is the trademark of the popular performer, Joan Baez does not strive to project an ingratiating image of herself. As she walks on stage she appears almost somnambulistic: her large, dark eyes are expressionless; her lean, Indian-like features, strangely immobile. She does not toss her long hair for effect, and her gestures are limited to long-fingered arpeggios on the strings of her guitar. A bass player who has accompanied her says, "She steps up there and opens her mouth and suddenly waves of love are going out all over the place. The funny thing is that she doesn't really *give* that much. She doesn't even seem to care whether the audience likes her or not." This is true: to the most frenzied applause, Miss Baez responds with nothing more than an occasional careless nod, but the listeners do not complain; they are partly hypnotized and partly intimidated by this unassuming girl, as though they were afraid she might decide not to sing for them again.

Off stage she is equally reticent (although she came to the Newport Festival in an old Cadillac hearse with her name painted on the side—her first and last theatrical stunt), insisting that she be interviewed only in her dressing room before a concert and shyly declining to make other appointments. For two years she turned down offers to go on tour; only recently did she realize that she could aid organizations such as UNESCO and CORE (Congress on Racial Equality) by appearing on their behalf.

Unlike folk musicologists who travel with tape recorders through rural tracts to search out obscure, authentic music, Miss Baez simply selects from what she hears or from what people send her, bringing a highly personal interpretation to the Anglo-American ballads for which she was best-known at the start of her career (for example, "Silver Dagger," "Mary Hamilton," "The Cherry Tree Carol"), to some carefully chosen spirituals and blues ("Virgin Mary," "House of the Rising Sun"), and to the country music that is her current interest ("Pal of Mine," "Old Blue"). Her "style" consists in not having a style, of allowing her voice to come through unadorned.

When she is criticized, it is for lack of vocal variation, but she can, in fact, change the sound of her voice radically. In the driving, rebellious import from Mexico, *"El Preso Numero Nueve,"* her normally lilting soprano switches to a dramatic lower register; and she can deliver a satirical and unexpectedly nasal version of that novel ethnic broadside, "Come On, Daddy, Let the Good Times Roll." Now a skillful instrumentalist, Miss Baez will sometimes put her guitar aside and sing unaccompanied; few other folk singers have interesting enough voices to do this successfully.

But Joan Baez is a phenomenon, a thoroughly natural yet polished and confident performer. The folk tradition is unself-consciously selective: the songs that last are the best songs; the same is true of the singers. JUDITH MILAN

66

The Man Who Cleaned Up
SHAKESPEARE

While Dr. Bowdler is long dead, his spirit of expurgating the Bard

lives on in our schools—though at the corner

drugstore pupils can get the real thing, and Henry Miller too

One of my poignant memories of high school is the day when in third-year English we began to read *Othello*. Our teacher, who may as well be called Miss Jones, had ordered a neat, single-volume edition of the play because, as she explained, it was so much nicer to have each of Shakespeare's works all by itself. The books arrived in the middle of a May morning, and it was decided that we would plunge right in. Miss Jones undertook to read the first act aloud to us, and we listened with considerable attention as she declaimed the lines the Bard had invented for the introduction of Iago and Roderigo.

Everything went smoothly until the part where the two conspirators are outside Brabantio's Venetian home, ready to reveal to the senator his daughter's elopement with Othello. Miss Jones had really caught the spirit of the scene by this time and was delivering Iago's speech with a venom I never would have thought her capable of:

> Zounds, sir, you're robb'd; for shame, put on your gown;
> Your heart is burst, you have lost half your soul;
> Even now, now, very now, an old black ram
> Is tupping your white ewe.

A dead silence fell upon the room. Outside, on a nearby branch, a bird chirped; through the wall I could faintly hear Miss Kenyon, in history class, going on about the Reformation. A slow flush had crept up Miss Jones's neck and was diffusing across her cheeks.

"Miss Jones," said a plaintive voice from the back of the room, "What does that mean? About the ram?"

It was, as they say, a good question. Miss Jones, who by this time had turned back to stare raptly at the title page, answered by announcing amid some confusion that a mistake had been made—this was *not* the edition of *Othello* she had ordered. And so the neat little volumes were collected again; and I, for one, gave up my copy reluctantly.

I thought of this episode recently when I encountered the famous edition of Shakespeare smugly put forth in 1818 by Dr. Thomas Bowdler, F.R.S., S.A.; *The Family Shakespeare,*

he called it: "In which nothing is added to the original text; but those words and expressions are omitted which cannot with propriety be read aloud in a family." I flipped through Volume VIII until I came to *Othello,* and sure enough, the old black ram was gone. It was clear to me that Dr. Bowdler and Miss Jones would have seen, if the expression may be pardoned, ewe to ewe.

A skimming perusal of the rest of the play provided several obvious samples of the sort of thing Bowdler thought too raw for the family circle. Totally absent were such touches of lyrical eroticism as, "Make love's quick pants in Desdemona's arms"; "They met so near with their lips, that their breaths embraced together"; and "He hath not yet made wanton the night with her, and she is sport for Jove." Dr. Bowdler could hardly pretend to his readers that sexual love had nothing to do with the plot of *Othello*; but he was going to make sure it was not presented as sport, spectator or otherwise.

It turns out, moreover, that "nothing is added to the original text" cannot be taken literally. Bowdler does add many words in the form of substitutions, and although these seldom amount to more than two or three at a time, the alteration they produce in Shakespeare's effect is often jarring. In that same opening scene of *Othello,* for instance, Iago lines out another famous metaphor to dazzle Brabantio, Dr. Bowdler, and Miss Jones: "I am one, sir, that comes to tell you your daughter and the Moor are now making the beast with two backs." Since this is in answer to Brabantio's question, "What profane wretch art thou?" Bowdler did not feel that he could dispense with it entirely; so he changed it to: "I am one, sir, that comes to tell you your daughter and the Moor are now together." This, of course, is not at all what Iago has come to tell, and such an impotent conclusion seems somewhat inadequate to explain Brabantio's fury at his midnight informer. After all, the family reader might conclude, perhaps Othello and Desdemona are just off in a gondola somewhere, holding hands.

The man who was first responsible for the systematic

By E. M. HALLIDAY

purification of Shakespeare—whose name, indeed, has become a synonym for genteel expurgation—came by his pious occupation all too legitimately. The atmosphere of the English family into which he was born, near Bath, on July 11, 1754, was inescapably moral. His mother had dabbled for years in religious poetry and essays, and she raised two daughters, Henrietta and Jane, to do likewise. Both of them, while failing to achieve matrimony, became popular authors of works on the Pleasures of Religion, the Advantages of Affliction, et cetera; and their elder brother, John, was also a best seller with his *Reform or Ruin* (1797), a pamphlet strenuously exposing the moral corruption of British society. Thomas Bowdler satisfied his father's wish by studying medicine at Edinburgh, but he had no taste for the profession and promptly gave it up upon receiving his inheritance in 1785. His concern, like that of his siblings, was more with the human soul than with its house of clay.

Settling down in London, Bowdler moved happily among the most polite and cultivated people of the 1780's. A frequent visitor at the bluestocking literary salons of Elizabeth Montagu and Hannah More, he seems, on the whole, to have preferred the company of ladies. This was good preparation for his task of pruning Shakespeare, and since his edition is dedicated to the memory of Mrs. Montagu, it may be assumed that what he changed or cut was what might have offended the ears of that paradigm of gentility.

It cannot be said that Bowdler came immaturely to the magnum opus that was to immortalize his name: he was sixty-four in 1818, when the first run of *The Family Shakespeare* came off the press. He had traveled widely in Europe, and in England had become well known for an active part in various social reclamation groups like the Proclamation Society—forerunner of the Society for the Suppression of Vice. The time was ripe for his project. The age of romanticism was well begun, and the swooning heroines of early nineteenth-century fiction were sentimentally in perfect phase with the audience Bowdler hoped to reach. Just over the horizon of history gleamed the Victorian era.

Although Bowdler is scarcely humble in his preface to *The Family Shakespeare,* he maintains a surface modesty. It is the peculiar advantage of literature, he points out, that unlike painting or sculpture, it can be modified without danger of permanent injury: the original work remains unimpaired and always available, even if the emendations "should immediately be consigned to oblivion." The risk of error therefore need not disturb the courageous reformer; nor should Shakespeare's acknowledged eminence over all other poets cause him to tremble. Even Homer nods; and even Shakespeare has his defects—principally a regrettable tendency to use lewd words and expressions. Bowdler's explanation of this fault falls back on stock eighteenth-century Shakespeare criticism: the Bard of Avon was an untutored genius, a child of Nature who warbled his native wood-notes with "unbridled fancy," insufficiently aware of the proper rules of art. On top of that, Shakespeare no doubt deliberately sauced up his creations "to gratify the bad taste of the age in which he lived." But, says Bowdler, "neither the vicious taste of the age, nor the most brilliant effusions of wit, can afford an excuse for profaneness or obscenity; and if these could be obliterated, the transcendent genius of the poet would undoubtedly shine with more unclouded lustre."

That they could be obliterated, and by himself, Bowdler felt highly confident. Like most censors he was perfectly convinced that his own taste was somehow in tune with the music of the spheres: where he found offense, surely all persons of sound moral judgment would also find offense. Behind his complacency lay the assumption of a Deity who had chosen to infuse into the Best People a practically infallible sense of what was right, what wrong. Just as litmus paper detects acid by turning red, a blush on a sensitive cheek would certainly indicate those passages where Shakespeare had gone awry. With his built-in detector as a guide, Bowdler was ready for action; when he finished, he doubted not of his success: "I hope I may venture to assure the parents and guardians of youth, that they may read the FAMILY SHAKESPEARE aloud in the mixed society of young persons of both sexes *sans peur et sans reproche.*" The Bayard of Avon had fulfilled his quest.

Looking back on the changes Bowdler made nearly a century and a half ago, the modern reader is likely to be impressed as much by what he left in as by what he took out. Fluctuations of taste are precarious. Words which today have acquired an unsavory aura failed to strike him as obnoxious: thus he allows Othello to call Desdemona a "whore," yet avoids the word "bawd" as if it were contagious. A society which, like ours today, considers it indecent for a mother to be seen nursing her baby in public would be unlikely to regard Bowdler's substitution of "teat" for "dug" (in *Romeo and Juliet*) as an improvement. Again, "His friend's with child by him," in *Measure for Measure,* sounds little different to the twentieth-century ear than Shakespeare's original "He hath got his friend with child"; evidently it was the word "got" that Bowdler could not stomach. And when, in the same play, he changes Claudio's "The stealth of our most mutual entertainment" to "The stealth of our most mutual intercourse," the switch seems to be in the direction of clinical specification rather than propriety.

Despite shifts in semantics and taste, however, these examples offer clues to Bowdler's sensibility. Two things he will not tolerate: the suggestion that sexual relations can be fun, and the suggestion that human beings belong to the animal kingdom. Out goes any patently joking reference to sex, like the marvelous foolery between Pompey and Elbow in *Measure for Measure;* out goes the Nurse's delighted account, in *Romeo and Juliet,* of her late husband's prediction that Juliet would "fall backward" when she had "more wit." Bowdler habitually changes "body" to "person"; he refuses to let Isabella, in *Measure for Measure,* call her brother a "beast"; and in Hamlet's celebrated catalogue of the characteristics of old men the one that gets dropped is "most weak hams." Pigs were pigs, but men, young or old, could not be allowed to have hams.

Like any alert censor, Bowdler took no chances with suspicious passages, even if he was not quite sure what they meant. It is doubtful that he fully understood (since editors still argue about their precise meaning) "groping for trouts in a peculiar river" (*Measure for Measure*) or "change the cod's head for the salmon's tail" (*Othello*), but he threw them out: they smelled, shall we say, fishy. Sometimes he slips in a way that one is tempted to describe as Freudian: for instance when he knocks out Hamlet's teasing question to Ophelia, "Lady, shall I lie in your lap?" and replaces it with the stage direction, "Laying [*sic*] down at Ophelia's feet." And sometimes connotations quite unsuspected when he made his careful emendations have cropped up in the intervening years to rob them of their dignity, as when he changes Iago's "twixt my sheets / He has done my office" to "in my bed / He has done me wrong." Shades of Frankie and Johnny! This is also a nice illustration of how ordinary words can pick up a connotative load through idiomatic use —a problem Bowdler was uncomfortably aware of. "No

words," he observed, "can be more harmless than the short words 'to do'; yet in the mouths of Pandarus and Cressida the words are unfit to be repeated." On that point, I might add, times have not changed too much: I remember my father's forbidding my sister to sing aloud the apparently innocent words of a popular ditty called "Let's Do It."

Bowdler's detergent labors met with great applause. His first edition sold out quickly, and by 1824 three more had appeared. There were a few cavilers, but they did not intimidate the editor; they were critics, he felt sure, "who do not appear to have made any inquiry into the merits or demerits of the performance, but condemn every attempt at removing indecency from Shakespeare." He nevertheless was at pains, in the preface to his fourth edition (1825), to defend his purpose and method at some length. One objection that had stung him was that Shakespeare could not be expurgated without injuring the dramatic structure of the plays, and this he set about to refute as smartly as he could.

"It is indeed a difficulty," Bowdler admits, "and a very great one, under which I labor, that it is not possible for me to state the words which I have omitted; but I think that I may adduce one instance, which, without offending the eye or the ear of modesty, will sufficiently . . . prove that a whole scene may be omitted, not only without injury, but with manifest advantage to the drama." The scene he is talking about, it develops, is the one in *Henry V,* Act III, where the French princess, Katharine, makes a lighthearted effort to learn a little English from her maid, Alice. It seems, as viewers of Sir Laurence Olivier's screen version will concede, a delicious interlude amidst the alarums, flourishes, and orations of a Shakespeare history; but its true and sole purpose, Bowdler assures us, is a dark one. It is no less than to introduce, "through the medium of imperfect pronunciation, the two most indecent words in the French language." The whole scene, therefore, can be chopped out not only to the advantage of morality but of dramatic structure.

It appears never to have occurred to Bowdler that hundreds of his readers would scurry to an untinkered version of *Henry V* to see what in the world those two French words might be. It is a fair guess that for a decade or so he gave that particular scene a secret vogue it had never previously enjoyed. For the ease of the present reader, let me remind him that the two words are Katharine's crude attempts to pronounce "foot" and "gown"—which may suggest little even to some who have spent years studying French. Yet Bowdler assumed that these words would be nastily meaningful to English ladies of Jane Austen's generation: at their mention, he says, "the princess is shocked, as every virtuous woman would be, if she were either here or elsewhere, to see them written, or hear them repeated."

Is it true that Bowdler's excisions and euphemisms seriously damage Shakespeare's plays? I think they do, and not merely from the point of view of dramaturgy or diction, but even more with respect to his matchless vitality. For my taste, Bowdler was deceived in supposing that he could remove whole scenes without violating dramatic structure,

DRAWINGS BY CHAS B. SLACKMAN

and that a change like watering down Hamlet's "Remorse-less, treacherous, lecherous, kindless villain!" to "Remorse-less, treacherous, unnatural villain!" was not an affront to poetry. He was much more deceived in depreciating Shake-speare's whole and steady vision of life in all its fullness. The role of sex in human affairs was not, for Shakespeare, something superficial and meretricious, to be exploited in his plays as a lure for prurient minds. It was of the essence. Like any other essential theme, it had its humorous high-lights as well as its tragic depths, and with the marvelous completeness which no other playwright has ever equaled, he displayed them all. "Purify" *Othello, Lear, Hamlet,* and a dozen others of their sexual overtones and specific pas-sages, and they lose half their meaning.

It must be admitted, indeed, that Bowdler himself seemed to become aware of this to some extent as he worked at his job of snipping and clipping. He confesses in his preface to the fourth edition that he is not entirely satisfied with *Othello, Measure for Measure,* and the two parts of *Henry IV:* they had proved too recalcitrant to his shears. From the latter he utterly banished Doll Tearsheet without a qualm; but he shows that he understood at least dimly that the Falstaff who remained when he was done with him was only a feeble shadow of the lusty rogue whose capon-stuffed belly presided at the sessions of the Boar's Head Tavern. It is a pity that Bowdler was unable to assimilate, instead of ex-purgating, Lucio's sage observation in *Measure for Measure:* "A little more lenity to lechery would do no harm . . . it is impossible to extirp it quite, friar, till eating and drinking be put down." As for *Othello,* it would seem that Bowdler found Shakespeare's searching portrayal of sexual jealousy rather overwhelming: he added a postscript to the play in which he suggested a slight change of plot that would make the alleged adultery of Cassio and Desdemona more believ-able. Thus we find the purse-lipped editor collaborating with Shakespeare in the dramatic representation of sexual intrigue.

When all is said and done, it may well be that history has been a bit unfair to Bowdler's memory. The verb which has grown out of his name is seldom used except contemptu-ously, and it is a cliché of reference books to describe him as a foolish bigot who made (as the *Dictionary of National Biography* puts it) "sad havoc" of Shakespeare's text. It was, to be sure, a pallid version that he offered the nineteenth century, drained of much of its living sap. Yet there is no doubt that he carried the great poet's work to an audience which otherwise would have been almost totally deprived of it. Algernon Charles Swinburne, certainly no prude, put it bluntly enough at the close of the century: "More nau-seous or foolish cant was never chattered than that which would deride the memory or depreciate the merits of Bowd-ler. No man ever did better service to Shakespeare than the man who made it possible to put him into the hands of in-telligent and imaginative children."

Today, when almost all moral censorship has been laughed out of our manners (and out of our courts and the Post Office as well), one would assume that bowdlerization was a thing of the past. Yet not so, when it comes to our precious young and Shakespeare. Miss Jones, apparently immortal, remains on Bowdler's side, and most school boards across the land stand squarely behind her. The Shakespeare texts chosen for official high school use in America today follow Bowdler's excisions pretty closely; they are, as a textbook editor put it recently when pressed, "lightly expurgated."

This leaves the imaginative child of our time still wonder-ing what Hamlet *really* said to Ophelia, or just why the Nurse in *Romeo and Juliet* has the reputation of being so bawdy. If he wants to find out, of course, he has only to walk to the nearest drugstore, where he can purchase, for little more than the cost of a sundae, a copy of Shakespeare alive with all its pristine impurity. Just possibly, too, he may notice a copy of *The Tropic of Cancer* on the stand, and be off into orbits that neither Dr. Bowdler nor Miss Jones ever dreamed of.

E. M. Halliday, who has taught literature at several uni-versities, recently joined the staff of AMERICAN HERITAGE.

Opposite: Nowhere else in the Moslem world was there anything like the Great Mosque of Córdoba, with its forest of ancient Roman columns supporting double arches of red brick and white stone. Begun in 785 and enlarged during the next two hundred years, it is now the cathedral.

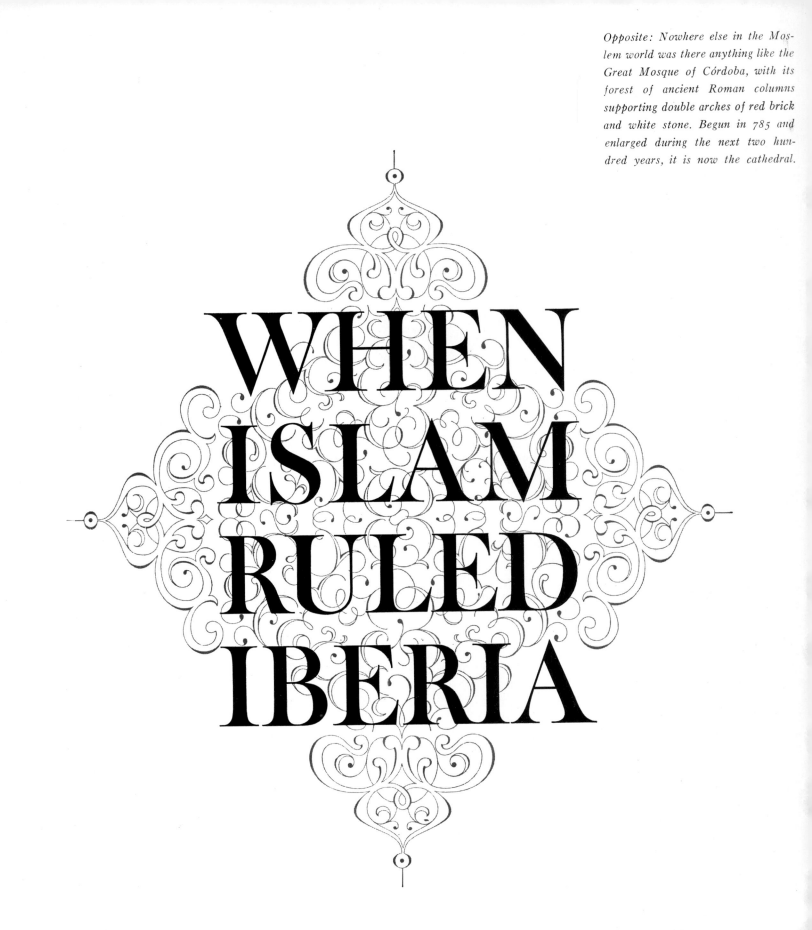

WHEN ISLAM RULED IBERIA

Less than a hundred years after they hurled themselves out of the desert, the Arabs were building in Spain a civilization that lasted almost eight centuries and cast the one bright ray of light into the Dark Ages of Europe

By GERALD BRENAN

ne morning in July, 711, a battle took place that decided the fate of Spain for more than five centuries. All the country south of the Pyrenees was then ruled by Visigoths, who had occupied it during the last years of the Roman Empire. But far away in the East a new power had arisen which, under the inspiration of a prophet called Mohammed, had overrun Syria, Mesopotamia, Persia, and Egypt. Exhilarated by their easy conquests, the armies of this militant new religion had marched on along the African coast till they reached Morocco. Here they had orders to stop, but the attraction of slaves and booty was too strong: Tarik, the military governor of Tangier, sent four hundred men across the Straits of Gibraltar to see what could be picked up. They returned with a cargo of beautiful women who so impressed Musa ibn Nusair, the caliph's governor in North Africa, that he ordered Tarik to take across a stronger contingent the following year.

Tarik landed with a small force, while Rodrigo, the Visigothic king, marched to encounter him with a much larger one. They met on the banks of the shallow lagoon of La Janda, close to Tarifa, and Rodrigo was defeated. Musa himself landed the next summer with another army, and within a couple of years most of the Iberian Peninsula had been occupied by the invaders.

The ramshackle but oppressive Visigothic regime had fallen, and a much more vital one had taken its place. Over the course of years the Moslems were to introduce into Spain the culture of the Alexandrian Greeks and the refine-ment of the Persians, creating a brilliant civilization that could compare with anything in the East. Yet their long occupation of the Peninsula was largely an interruption of Spanish history. The Christian state that emerged after centuries of fighting was, as one might expect, a militant state fortified by a militant church. The Spaniards acquired the special character they have had since the Middle Ages not so much by learning from the Moors as by crusading against them, and the culture they eventually adopted was borrowed in all but a few details from France and Italy.

At first, however, the Moslem invaders had it entirely their own way. In every city of Spain they found people who welcomed them. This was partly the result of their tolerant and easygoing policy: everyone who submitted was allowed to keep his estates; the privileges of the great feudal lords were confirmed by special treaties; and there was complete religious toleration, except that the Christians had to pay a poll tax from which the Moslems were exempted. So many Spaniards went over to the new faith in order to escape taxation that within a hundred years of the Arab conquest most of the population professed the creed of Mohammed.

Yet the Moslems did not at first bring settled government. For forty years the country was torn by civil strife. The old feuds of the desert broke out again on Spanish soil, with the men of northern Arabia lined up against those of Yemen. A raid into France to loot the tomb of Saint Martin of Tours was repelled by Charles Martel in 732 at Poitiers, the far-

thest limit of the Moslem advance (see above). More important for Spain, a center of Christian resistance appeared in the mountains of Asturias: the Visigoth chieftain Pelayo, hiding in a cave with his thirty followers, marks the beginning of the *Reconquista*. Soon his successor, Alfonso, was carving out a kingdom in the northwest, where the wet, forested country held no appeal for the Moslems. From now on there were to be two Spains, perpetually at war with each other.

Meanwhile, great changes were taking place in the East: the Umayyad caliphate of Damascus had been undermined by the rise of the Shi'ite and Kharijite heresies, and in 750 it fell and was succeeded by that of the Abbasids at Baghdad. The new caliph caught and beheaded every male member of the Umayyad family except one. This was Abd al-Rahman, who, after a series of hairbreadth adventures, escaped to Morocco. From here, on the invitation of one of the factions, he crossed to Spain in 755 and the next year was proclaimed emir of al-Andalus, as the Moslems called their Spanish kingdom. He was twenty-five and his real difficulties were only beginning.

Abd al-Rahman reigned for thirty-two years. Every one of those years was filled with risings and insurrections, made not by the conquered Spaniards but by his ungovernable compatriots. Even his own family conspired against him, and he needed all his energy and ruthlessness to maintain his position. He was a sad man who always dressed in white, the color of his house, and his private tastes lay in gardens and plants which, with the nostalgia of the exile, he im-

ported from his native Syria. But we owe him a debt of gratitude for building the Great Mosque at Córdoba (see page 73). It was the finest Arab mosque of the time and marks a great breach with all previous styles of building. Art progresses by having new problems to solve. In this case the difficulty to be overcome lay in the shortness of the old Roman columns he had decided to re-use. The roof needed to be much higher, so above the columns the architect erected a double tier of horseshoe arches; this in turn led to another discovery, the intersecting arch. Most of the original features of Spanish Arab architecture derive from this innovation, which has a special interest for us because architecture is one of the few things in which Christian Spain was influenced by the Moslems. During the Middle Ages, Moorish and Christian craftsmen often worked side by side, just as they did in the potteries, producing the so-called Mudejar style; and when later on, baroque succeeded the classical style of the Renaissance, in Spain as elsewhere, the great richness and complexity of Spanish baroque wall surfaces and chapels suggests an Oriental attitude, even though there was no direct influence.

Abd al-Rahman was succeeded by his son, Hisham I. His short reign (788–796) is notable for the introduction of the Malikite school of theology. This is the most conservative of the four orthodox Islamic schools, and in Spain it became more conservative than anywhere else. Under the direction of the *fakihs*, or men of religion, it led to a speculative paralysis that down to the end of the caliphate (in

The ruined mill opposite is one of an estimated five thousand built along the Guadalquivir by Moslem engineers during the tenth century. From the river, "placid as a stream of milk," they drew both power and water for irrigation. But the most imposing structure of the period was Madinat al-Zahra, the palace-city built by Abd al-Rahman III outside Córdoba. All that remains of what was then the most luxurious court in Western Europe are its crumbling foundations (right) and fragments like the marble cistern below.

1027) prevented any discussion on philosophic or scientific questions. Every work on these subjects was regarded as heretical. Since the Moslem world elsewhere was being racked at this time by religious controversies, the Malikite orthodoxy helped to keep Spain quiet and so was supported by the emirs in spite of their being themselves inclined to tolerance. One is reminded of the rigid doctrinal control exercised later by the Spanish Inquisition in order to keep out Protestantism.

The next two emirs had very different reigns. The first, al-Hakam I, was a pleasure-loving man who enjoyed hunting cranes by the river, playing ball, and listening to recitations of poetry; but he incurred the enmity of the *fckihs* because he drank wine, and they stirred up against him riots and rebellions that he put down with great severity. This allowed a long and peaceful reign (822–852) to his successor, Abd al-Rahman II. The work of consolidation now seemed to be over and the emirate of Córdoba took its place among the leading states of the world. It had at least no rivals, for the Abbasid caliphate in Baghdad was in rapid decay, North Africa had split up into independent states, and Europe was sunk in the lowest depths of the Dark Ages.

In contrast to this, the life of the court and aristocracy at Córdoba was one of refinement and luxury. Exquisite brocades, gold and ivory caskets, rare books, and accomplished singing girls were imported from the East, while the Emir's agents had bought up most of Harun al-Rashid's jewelry.

The person who taught the Córdoban court and aristocracy how to display wealth with elegance was the Iraqi musician Ziryab. He was the best singer of his day and is said to have known more than a thousand songs by heart, each with its appropriate tune. He invented a lute that had five strings instead of four and set up a conservatory in which the "Andalusian" music that may be heard today in the gardens of Fez—it is really Persian—acquired its form. But he was more than a musician; he was a man of wide culture and discriminating taste. Finding the customs of the Córdobans crude and provincial, he decided to reform them. With the encouragement of the Emir, he laid down rules as to what clothes should be worn in each season, changed hair styles, and taught new ways of cooking and serving food. Thus we find him introducing asparagus and substituting drinking glasses for gold or silver goblets and replacing tablecloths of stamped leather with damask ones.

The history of Moslem states has a peculiar rhythm of its own: a generation or two of stable government is regularly followed by a period of chaos. Autocratic rule is commonly subject to these explosions, which break out when the discontent due to bad trade or to a failure of crops is fanned by local disaffection or by religious fanaticism. So now, after Abd al-Rahman II's death in 852, thirty years of utter anarchy set in. The mountainous region of the south rose under a guerrilla leader from Ronda, and all the great cities rebelled and declared themselves independent. The emirate of Córdoba seemed about to disappear when, in 912, a young man of twenty-one succeeded to the throne. This was Abd al-Rahman III, who was perhaps the greatest ruler Spain was ever to know.

It took him twenty years of hard fighting to reimpose his will on the country. After that he had to contain the Christian states of the north and to assert himself in Morocco, which had been conquered by the Fatimid dynasty that ruled in North Africa and Egypt. It was not till 929 that he felt himself strong enough to take the next step and to assume the title of caliph, Commander of the Faithful. This was possible because the caliphate at Baghdad had by now sunk to a shadow.

Córdoba at this time was a city of well over half a million inhabitants. That is to say, it was a little larger than Fez in Morocco is today. The general appearance of its streets must have been very similar, but it was a place of far greater wealth, and its Moslem aristocracy, hidden away in their palaces and gardens, lived in ease and luxury. In addition to the Great Mosque, which had now been enlarged, there were seven hundred smaller mosques and oratories and nine hundred public baths. But the court was the center of everything, and to get an idea of what it was like one must look at the new palace that Abd al-Rahman III put up a few miles outside the city (see page 77).

Madinat al-Zahra he called it, after a harem favorite. It took thirteen years to build because it was not only a palace but an administrative center that had to house a considerable population. The palace apartments contained fourteen thousand male domestics, all of them Franks, and six thousand women, including slaves, living in the harem. As an indication of the cost of supplying this establishment, we are told that twelve thousand loaves of bread were brought in every day merely to feed the fish in the ponds. The style of decoration was as lavish as anything to be seen at that time in Constantinople or Baghdad. Four thousand marble columns were employed for the mosque and for the various arcades, while the walls of the principal apartments were lined with green and rose marble that had been imported from Tunisia. The ceilings were gilded and the doors inlaid with silver, ivory, and precious stones. But the room known as the Hall of the Caliphs surpassed all the rest. Its vaulted ceiling was encrusted with mosaics, its windows were of translucent alabaster, and it was entered by eight doors paneled with glass. In the center there was a huge marble basin filled with quicksilver. A mechanical device enabled a slave to agitate it; when that happened the whole room seemed to be turning in circles and throwing out spokes of light.

It was in this hall that Abd al-Rahman received the embassies of foreign nations. One came from Emperor Otto of Germany and another from the Byzantine emperor,

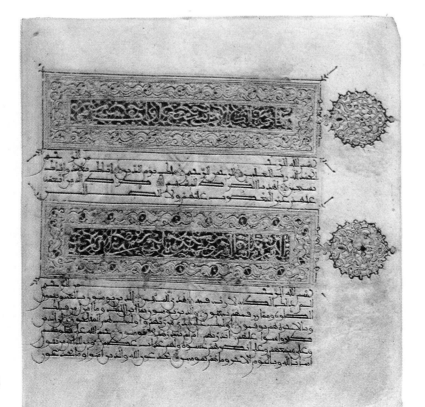

Left: The Koran was the basic textbook in Moslem education, and this page from a fourteenth-century copy made in Granada attests to the high art of the Andalusian scribes. Granada was the last Moslem state in Spain, not reconquered until 1492.

Opposite: Averroës, the great twelfth-century Córdoban physician and philosopher, is famous for his commentaries on Aristotle, but this Latin manuscript anachronistically shows him (left) discussing dietary abstinence with Porphyry, a third-century Greek.

78

Constantine Porphyrogenitus. To reach the Caliph they had to ride for four miles between rows of armed and mounted soldiers and then to pass on foot through room after room spread with rare Oriental carpets and hung with silk brocades. At the end they saw the Caliph seated on his throne, with his eight sons and his viziers and chamberlains standing on either side of him, and looking, as Otto's ambassador wrote, like an inaccessible divinity. On another occasion old Queen Tota, her son King Garcia of Navarre, and her grandson Sancho the Fat, deposed king of León, arrived and prostrated themselves before him. The Caliph had sent Sancho a Jewish doctor to cure him of his fatness, and now that he was thin again he had come to beg for an army to restore him to his throne.

It can be imagined what an effect these receptions had on the poor monarchs and ambassadors from the north. Europe was now touching its lowest level of misery and squalor, so that to a German or a Basque the court of Córdoba must have seemed as dazzling as Paris would have been fifty years ago to a Mongol from the Asiatic steppes. Yet it should be remembered that everything the caliphate could show—ceremonies, institutions, objects of luxury and display, palaces, libraries—had been borrowed from Damascus or Baghdad. There had been a complete break with the Roman and Visigothic world and, if we except the architecture of the Great Mosque, nothing new in the arts and refinements of life had made its appearance. A cultivated Iraqi or Egyptian would have found Córdoba dull and provincial.

However, there was one exception to the Oriental color of al-Andalus, and that lay in the language. The upper classes spoke most readily the debased Latin, mixed with Arabic words, that was growing into Spanish. The emirs and caliphs learned it in the nursery, for their mothers, like most of the women in the harem, were Galicians or Basques. For this reason the caliphs had blue eyes and fair hair.

Abd al-Rahman III died in 961 after a forty-nine year reign. He was a man of great presence and majesty who surrounded himself with Byzantine ceremonial yet was frank and easy with his friends. His generosity and benevolence made him well-liked, and he had achieved all that he had set himself to do. Yet it seems that he did not regard himself as happy. After his death a paper was found on which he had noted those days of his reign on which he had been completely happy and free from care: they numbered only fourteen.

His son al-Hakam II was forty-six when he succeeded to the throne. He was a bookish man with a loud voice, a beaked nose, and short legs, who suffered from poor health. For this reason he had spent the years before his succession in assembling and reading a library of 400,000 volumes. Few libraries in Europe at this time contained more than five hundred, but the manufacture of paper had recently been introduced from China to Iraq and paper books cost only a fraction of vellum ones. Arabic script, too, is a sort of shorthand, so that a vast spate of literary, theological, and philosophical works, among them translations from Greek, had begun to appear in the Near East. Many private persons in Córdoba also acquired large libraries; the standard of education in the city was so high that almost everyone could read and write at a time when, in northern Europe, few princes or emperors could read a line.

TEXT CONTINUED ON PAGE 82

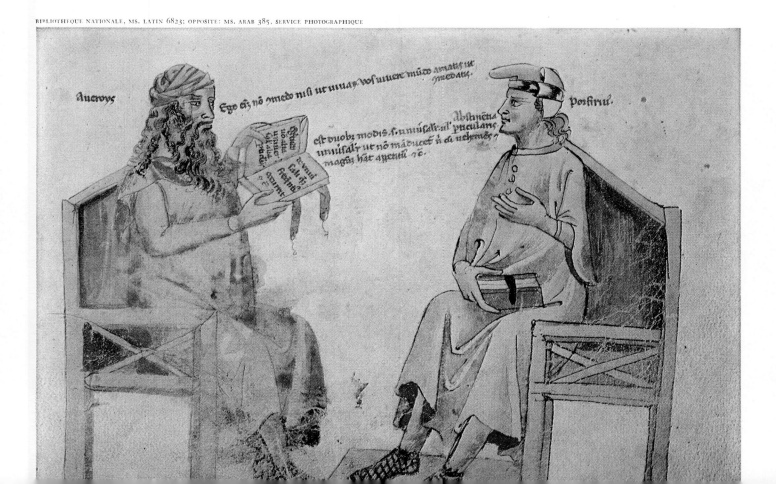

MOSLEM GIFTS TO THE WEST

Left: This is a page from a thirteenth-century French copy of the Toledan Tables—astronomical charts that were drawn up originally in the eleventh century by Arzachel (al-Zarkali) of Toledo and used for five hundred years by the astronomers and navigators of Western Europe for their calculations. Below: In the same way, later cartographers based their maps on the monumental atlas of al-Idrisi, who was educated in Córdoba but worked at the court of the Norman king of Sicily, Roger II. His map of 1154 (this is a modern German facsimile, reproduced upside down for clarity) shows most of the known world, from Spain at left to China at extreme right. Opposite, left: A page from Euclid's Elements is shown as translated by the twelfth-century English scholar Adelard of Bath from Arabic into Latin. Before the Renaissance, this is probably how most of the Greek texts reached Western Europe. Opposite, upper right: The greatest physician of Moslem Spain was Abulcasis, whose surgical treatise, written in the late tenth century, was used throughout Europe after it was translated by Gerard of Cremona two hundred years later. At the top is a diagram for anchoring loose teeth with gold wires, and immediately under it the Latin adaptation; beneath are Arabic and Latin versions of a cauterizing instrument for stomach ailments, and the pattern of burns to be made on the skin. Lower right: The portable astrolabe, perfected by the Arabs and introduced by them to Europe, grew into the mariner's astrolabe that Spanish explorers used to open up a new world.

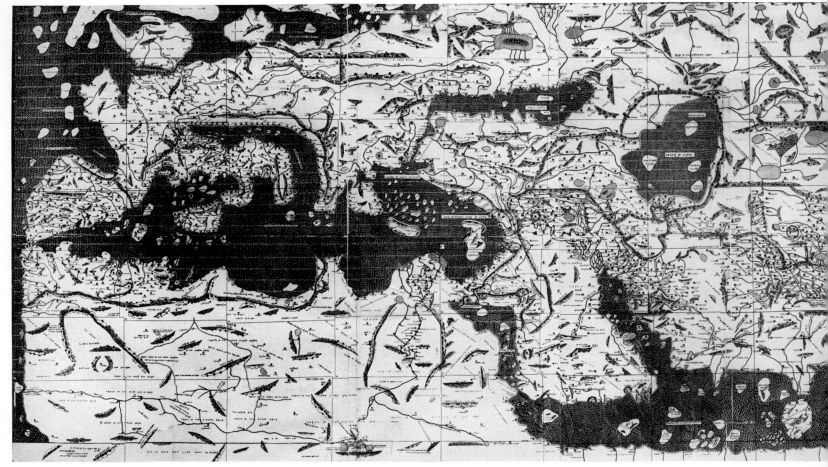

MOSLEM GIFTS TO THE WEST

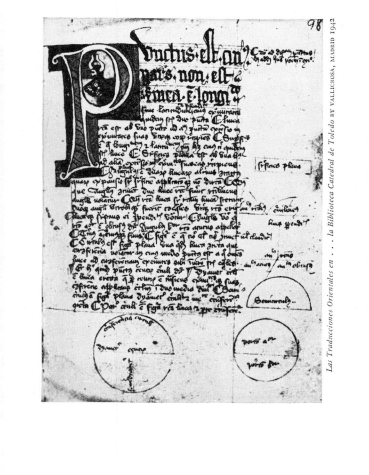

98

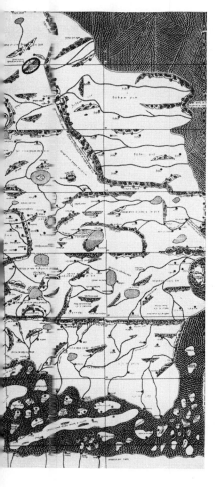

TEXT CONTINUED FROM PAGE 79

Al-Hakam II's reign showed a steady advance both in literary culture and in the crafts that minister to luxury. Córdoba ceased to depend on the East for its gold- and silverwork, its carved ivory, its fine cottons and silk brocades, and began to excel in the curing and tooling of leather. The old English word "cordwain," now replaced by "cordovan," preserves a memory of this. In agriculture, too, new plants were introduced—rice, sugar cane, cotton, the date palm, and the pomegranate. (Sweet oranges and lemons came in later.) Mulberry trees were planted in great numbers to feed the silkworms, and the area of land under artificial irrigation was greatly extended. Thus the plains of Valencia, Granada, and Málaga were being transformed into the rich oases one sees today, while in the cities, gardens were laid out with roses, Madonna lilies, and sweet-smelling herbs, edged with borders of rosemary or box. In northern Europe there were as yet no gardens.

After a reign of fifteen years al-Hakam II died, in 976, leaving a child of twelve, Hisham II, to succeed him. The real ruler, however, was not to be Hisham but an ambitious court official, Ibn Abi Amir, who is best known by the title he later took of al-Mansur, "the Victorious," which in Spanish became Almanzor. By seducing Hisham's Basque mother, he was able to raise himself to the position of chief minister. Then, to conciliate the *fakihs,* he ordered all the books in al-Hakam II's library that treated of science or philosophy to be destroyed; after which, to secure the army, he married the daughter of the powerful frontier general Ghalib. But the critical moment of Hisham's coming of age was approaching. Fortunately for Almanzor, the young Caliph was a weak creature who had been brought up in the harem and was alleged to be prematurely enfeebled by sexual indulgence. He was therefore easily persuaded to delegate the management of public affairs to his chief minister on the grounds that he wished to give himself up to religious exercises. So after suppressing an uprising by his father-in-law, Ghalib, Almanzor became the sole power in the country.

His first act was to give orders that his name should be mentioned immediately after the Caliph's in the mosques. This gave him the treatment of emir. He then married a daughter of the Christian king of Navarre, who paid him a visit in Córdoba, prostrated himself humbly, and kissed his feet. Ten years later Almanzor took a third wife, a daughter of the king of León. Meanwhile he had built himself a new palace and chancellery just outside Córdoba. Paraphrasing the name of Abd al-Rahman III's palace, he called it Madinat al-Zahira, "the brilliant city," and all the offices of the government were housed there. The older palace-city then became almost deserted, for Hisham had been removed to a fortress next to the Great Mosque in Córdoba.

But it is as a military commander, "the Scourge of the Christians," that Almanzor acquired his reputation. He began by reorganizing the army, increasing the number of the Berber and Frankish mercenaries, and reducing the strength of the native Andalusian levies. Then he pacified Morocco, extending his influence as far as Fez. He was now free to give all his attention to the Christian states in the north of Spain. Twice every year he led an army of from thirty to sixty thousand men across the frontier, capturing and sacking cities, cutting down trees, and bringing back as slaves the inhabitants he caught. Barcelona, León, Coimbra, Zamora, and Burgos were all taken by him and then burned and destroyed. But Almanzor's crowning exploit was his raid on the shrine of Saint James at Santiago de Compostela. After Rome it was the most famous pilgrimage place in Europe, and he knew that its destruction would send a wave of terror and anger through the Christian world. Marching northward, therefore, along the Portuguese coast, so that his fleet could provision him, he reached the city without opposition and found it abandoned by its inhabitants. He demolished it thoroughly, but spared the tomb of Saint James and the solitary monk who guarded it. Then, carrying with him the doors and the bells of the basilica, he returned to Córdoba. Five years later he was dead. A monk of Burgos recorded it tersely in his chronicle: "In 1002 Almanzor died and was buried in Hell."

These enormously expensive expeditions that the caliphs and Almanzor led across the Christian frontier were not aimed at conquest. No attempt was ever made to gain and occupy fresh territory. They were simply razzias, or raids, made in fulfillment of the command of the Prophet to carry on a holy war against the infidel. They had also the secondary purposes of raising the prestige of the ruler and of capturing slaves. The great prosperity of al-Andalus in Almanzor's time was partly due to the low price of slaves. Yet although these raids were so ruthlessly conducted—all prisoners taken on the battlefield were put to the sword, all cities were sacked, all men, women, and children who could be gathered in were carried off into slavery—there were at the same time close and often friendly relations between the people of the two religions. In al-Andalus itself there was complete religious toleration, and Moslems and Christians intermarried freely. There was some trade across the frontiers, conducted by Jews, and the people of the north imitated the manners and dress of the Moslems. Most surprising of all to our minds, the kings of León and Navarre sometimes enlisted the help of Moslem armies in their civil wars, while in Almanzor's raid on Santiago we read of a number of Leónese counts flocking to his standard and helping him in his assault on the holy shrine. Religion to the men of that day was one thing; war with the profit and honor it brought was another.

Almanzor was succeeded in power by his eldest son, who died after a reign of six years, and then pandemonium broke out. During this period the feeble caliph-in-name-only, Hisham II, was forced to abdicate; a great-grandson

TEXT CONTINUED ON PAGE 87

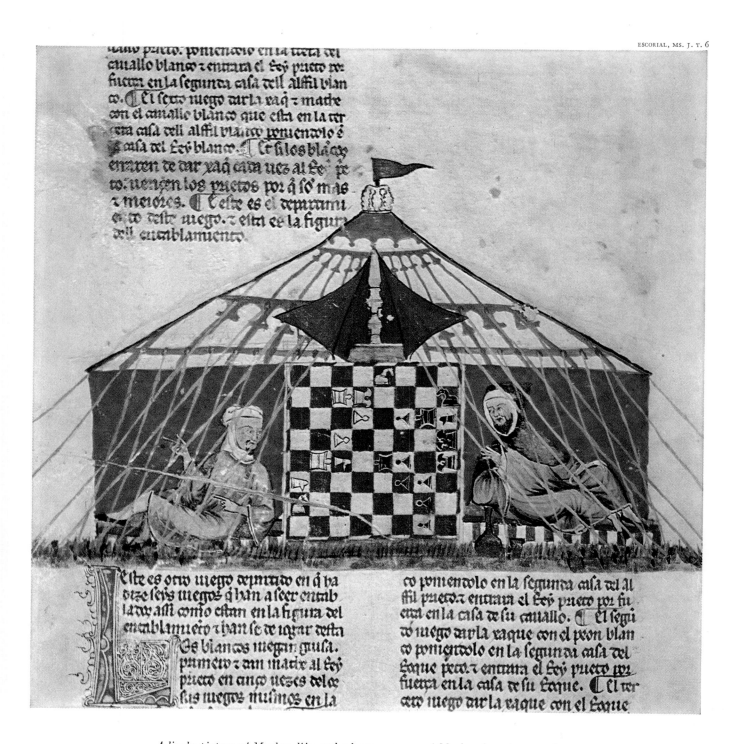

A lively picture of Moslem life, and a large measure of Moslem learning, was pre-served for Christian Spain by a thirteenth-century scholar-king of Castile and León—Alfonso X, el Sabio ("the Wise"). From his Book of Chess, *written in Galician (and the first description of the game in a European tongue), comes this image of two burnoosed chieftains pondering a problem in their tent. Overleaf and on the two following pages are three miniatures from another of his works, the* Cantigas de Santa Maria, *a collection of old poems set to music.*

*A twelfth-century governor of Seville holds a council of war in its fortified castle,
the Alcázar. At this time Moslem Spain was ruled by the Almohads, a Moroccan
dynasty, who enclosed their towns in jagged walls much like those depicted here.*

Another illustration from the same Cantiga as the preceding one shows the Moslems out on a military expedition. Their conical tents were often luxurious, although it is unlikely that their cavalry ever operated in such close formation.

These twelfth-century Spanish Moslem warships show some details borrowed from the Byzantines and some from the Normans, who at this time ruled in neighboring Sicily. For speed they depended on the 130 galley slaves at the oars.

of Abd al-Rahman III was made caliph in his place; and contending factions sacked and demolished, within a few months of each other, first the Madinat al-Zahira (so completely that no trace of it remains) and then the Madinat al-Zahra. The latter was the work of rebellious Berber mercenaries who marched back from the frontier and, after destroying al-Zahra, laid siege to the city. At the end of a year and a half it was starved into submission and the Berber troops poured in, looting the palaces and putting the inhabitants to the sword. But the Berbers had no wish to remain in Córdoba. The caliphate was finished, so they obliged the puppet whom they had put on the throne to make over to them the provinces of Granada and Jaén. Other Berbers from Africa occupied Málaga and the hill country around; the Slavs, as the Frankish mercenaries were called, took the east coast from Almería to Valencia; and the Moslem governors of Seville, Badajoz, Toledo, and Saragossa each proclaimed their independence. Córdoba settled down to be a republic, ruled by its Arab aristocracy, and the twenty years of anarchy known as the *fitna* were over.

Moslem Spain had now broken up into some thirty independent states, and one would have expected that the high standard of culture and learning which had developed during the caliphate would decline. In fact, the opposite happened. The Taifa kingdoms, as they were called, saw a flowering of literature and science that makes it possible to compare them to the Italian cities of the Renaissance. For the rulers of these new states, always in competition with one another, culture was an article of prestige; and so they lavished their money on libraries and *objets d'art* and on salaries to poets, philosophers, and mathematicians. The *fakihs*, who had lost much of their influence, had to bow to this. Thus, while the states where the Berbers had settled remained backward, Seville, Córdoba, Almería, Toledo, Badajoz, and Saragossa became centers where the arts and sciences were enthusiastically cultivated.

Poetry had always been the chief art form of the Arabs: there were great poets in Arabia before Mohammed's day. The caliphs of Córdoba had not only written poems themselves but had maintained a body of professional poets at their court (Almanzor is said never to have gone on a campaign without taking at least forty with him). But this poetry had been of poor quality. Now, however, a number of eminent poets appeared whose work could compare with anything that was being written in the East. Among them we may mention Ibn Hazm, a Córdoban of Spanish descent who also wrote a remarkable prose work on the psychology of love, as well as a comparative history of religion. And there was King al-Mutamid of Seville, whose tragic story has been related by Reinhart Dozy in his *Spanish Islam*. Now this, it will be remembered, is the period in which Provençal poetry was springing up in the south of France. Although there can be no question of any direct influence, it seems

AL-ANDALUS
BEFORE
THE RECONQUEST

Al-Maqqari's History of the Mohammedan Dynasties in Spain, *compiled in the early seventeenth century, preserves this lively eyewitness account by a thirteenth-century predecessor whose own books have been lost:*

"The inhabitants of Andalus," says Ibnu Sa'id, "dress somewhat differently from their Moslem brethren of Asia. . . . Even the people who use turbans follow a fashion of their own, and seem entirely to disregard the multifarious shapes used by people of rank and distinction in other Moslem states; so if an eastern Arab happens to come among them, wearing a turban in the Syrian or Hejazi fashion—and large high things they are, looking like towers—they will show great astonishment, and appear much struck with the novelty; but instead of admiring its shape and structure, they will burst out laughing, and jest at the expense of the wearer, for in general the Andalusians are very slow in adopting the fashions of other nations, and neither admire nor like anything but their own. They are also the cleanest people on earth in what regards their person, dress, beds, and in the interior of their houses; indeed, they carry cleanliness to such an extreme that it is not an uncommon thing for a man of the lower classes to spend his last dirhem in soap instead of buying food. . . ."

". . . Most [cities] are strongly fortified, and surrounded with walls, as a protection against the incursions of the enemy; some, even, will be found so strong by nature, or so well fortified by art, as to have been besieged by the Christians during twenty years without falling into their hands . . . for although it is true that at the time I write the enemy of God has penetrated far into the heart of Andalus, and considerably diminished the dominions of the Moslems, yet there are still remaining in the hands of the true believers cities like Seville, Granada, Malaga, Almeria, and others, ruling over extensive and populous districts, full of cities and towns, and provided with sufficient strength to resist and defeat, with God's help and assistance, all the attacks of the unbelievers."

Alas! the bright hopes of this holy man have been blighted, and his good wishes frustrated, for God Almighty had decreed that the contrary should happen, and that the worshipers of the crucified should everywhere subdue and overpower his own servants. Such was the will of God—Him who can change sorrow into joy, and pain into delight—the high! the great! May He permit in his infinite wisdom that the words of Islam resound again in Andalus, and that its present inhabitants be annihilated and destroyed!

likely that the idea that writing love poetry was a proper occupation for courts emanated from al-Andalus, and with it, perhaps, came a certain new attitude toward women. One of the causes of the ending of the Dark Ages was the discovery that the Moslem countries possessed a more refined and luxurious style of living than northern Europe and the desire of the feudal lords to raise more money so as to emulate it.

Philosophy developed for the most part a little later, in the twelfth century. Here the famous names are Avempace, Averroës, Ibn Tufail, and Ibn al-Arabi, to which must be added the Jewish philosophers Avicebrón and Maimonides. It was not a very original philosophy, for it consisted mainly of adaptations and combinations of Aristotelian and Neoplatonist ideas; but when it reached the Schoolmen of the north, it made a strong impact. Astronomy and medicine were also much practiced, but again with little advance on the work of the Alexandrian Greeks. Arithmetic, on the other hand, was more or less a creation of the Arabs—although they made little progress with it until they imported the notation we use today, including the sign for zero, from India.

The Taifa kingdoms lasted a bare sixty years. They were too weak to hold back the advancing Christians. Unwillingly, therefore, they called in the new power that had arisen in Morocco. Known as the Almoravids, these camel-riding Berbers from the Sahara lived on dates and veiled their faces (as their descendants, the Tuaregs, still do): they were recent converts to Islam and therefore full of zeal and fanaticism. Their emir, Yusuf, landed in Spain, cut to pieces the Castilian army that had marched to meet him, and then mopped up the Taifa kingdoms. The poets had to stop writing because there was no one to pay them their pensions, and the philosophers had to go into exile because the *fakihs* hated them. After the death of Yusuf there was a little more latitude, but Spanish Moslem culture had now to live on the impetus it drew from the past rather than on any new stimulus. And when Ferdinand III of Castile captured Córdoba in 1236 and Seville in 1248, Moslem rule in al-Andalus was over. Only the small kingdom of Granada remained.

But before this happened a very important thing for European culture had taken place. In 1084, just before the Almoravids crossed over to Spain, Alfonso VI of León and Castile had occupied Toledo. To bring the Spanish church into line with the Roman, he had given the most important posts in it to monks of the Benedictine order of Cluny. They, being Frenchmen, were deeply interested in Scholastic philosophy, and so the next archbishop of Toledo, Raymond, set up an institution for translating the Arab

During their entire time in Spain—almost eight hundred years—the Moslems were at war with the Christians along their borders. Moorish battle standards might proclaim "Victory is assured" (right), but it was not: the Christians inched ahead on the tide of awakening nationalism, and kept it moving by turning the heroes of the struggle into legends. In the late eleventh century this process produced one of the monuments of European literature, The Song of Roland—*a fanciful account of a foray into Spain by Charlemagne some three hundred years earlier. It exalts the deeds of the warrior Roland, shown rallying his troops in this fourteenth-century version (far left). More famous still was Rodrigo Díaz de Bivar, "El Cid," who has been celebrated as the national hero of Spain in song, epic, drama, sculpture (the statue at left stands in Burgos), and now the movies. Actually, he fought on both sides, and in behavior was almost as much Moslem as Christian.*

TOLEDO CATHEDRAL; OVERLEAF LEFT: FRANCISCO ONTANON; RIGHT: BRASSAI

and Jewish philosophers into Latin. This was done by Spanish Jews, who were often trilingual; and in this way a large number of books, including Arab translations of Aristotle, became available about 1150 to Western Europe. They arrived just when the need for them was greatest, and Avicebrón's *Well of Life* and Averroës's commentaries on Aristotle, to name only two, set off the great movement in Western philosophy that culminated in Albertus Magnus, Thomas Aquinas, and Duns Scotus. Other and more accurate translations followed, under the supervision of the Scottish alchemist and Arabic scholar Michael Scot, and works on medicine, astronomy, and mathematics were among them.

Here again it was mainly Greek science that the Arabs passed on. Their great physicians, Avicenna and Avenzoar, whose names were household words in the Middle Ages, introduced the system of Hippocrates, Dioscorides, and Galen. It was not a very useful system, for it was based on the false theory of the four humors; the Arabs, though they had brought in from India some new and valuable drugs, had neglected to pursue the Alexandrian practice of dissection, which might have led them to a better understanding of the functions of the bodily organs. The skill of their doctors was really founded on clinical experience, little of which found its way into their learned treatises. In the same way, Arab

TEXT CONTINUED ON PAGE 92

Overleaf: By the middle of the fourteenth century the once Moslem city of Toledo had been under Christian domination for three hundred years. This period gave rise to the blend of Christian and Moslem decoration known as the Mudejar style. The city's finest example is paradoxically the synagogue El Tránsito, where inscriptions in Hebrew are combined with latticed Moslem windows and, in the exquisitely worked plaster foliage below them, the arms of Catholic León and Castile. Following page: A cathedral bell now hangs in the top of the Giralda tower in Seville where once the voice of the muezzin called the faithful to prayer. Below it extends the Patio of the Oranges with its intricate pattern of irrigation channels for watering the trees. The Patio was originally the forecourt of the mosque and the Giralda its minaret. They were built by the Almohads late in the twelfth century and were incorporated in the fabric of the cathedral some two centuries afterward.

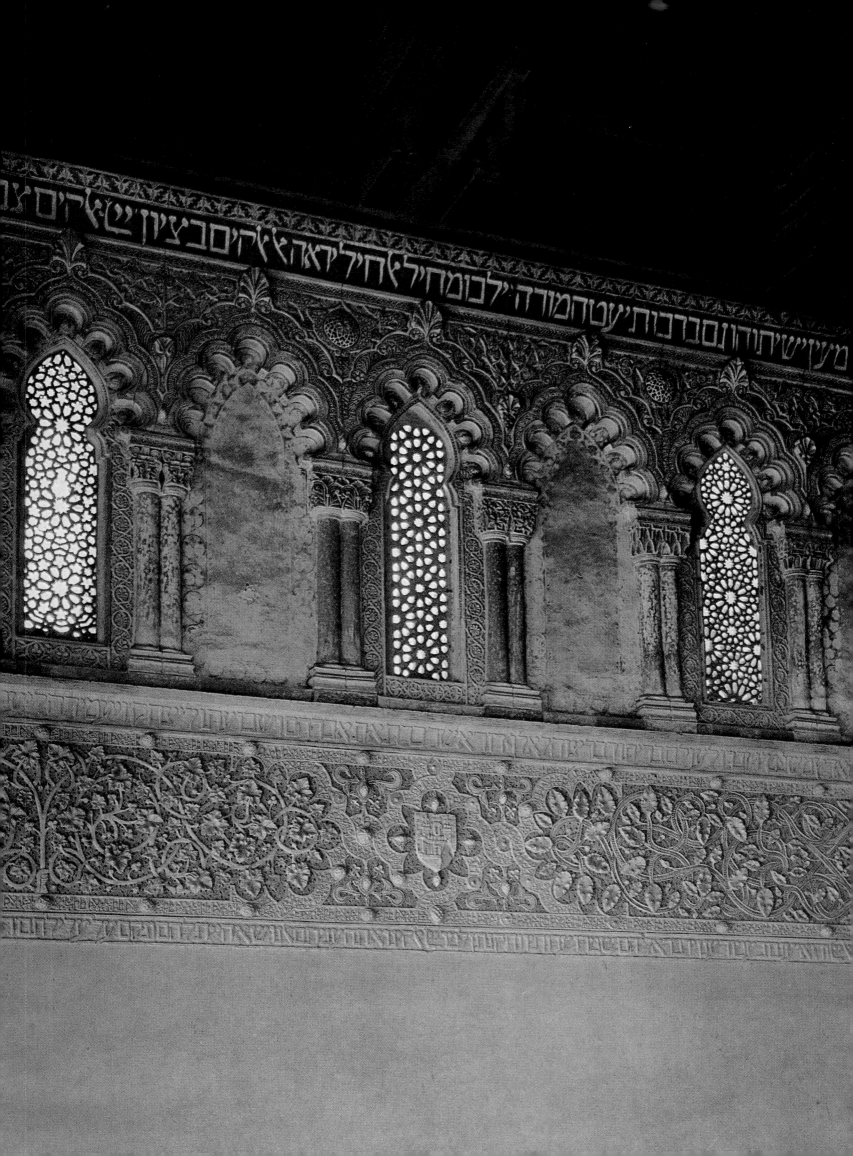

TEXT CONTINUED FROM PAGE 89

astronomy was based almost entirely on Ptolemy's *Almagest,* which Gerard of Cremona translated from Arabic into Latin about 1170. But Indian advances in trigonometry, as well as the more exact observations of their own astronomers, had enabled the Arabs to plot the movements of the stars and planets with greater accuracy; and for this reason the Tables of Arzachel of Toledo became the classic work on astronomy for the peoples of northern Europe and so prepared the way for Copernicus and Tycho Brahe.

Thus we see Spanish Islam passing on its acquisitions to a more creative and energetic world just as it was coming to an end itself (though the Berber kingdom of Granada lingered on till 1492, it had nothing to offer to other peoples). Then in 1610 the Moriscos, as the Moors who had now been forcibly converted to Christianity were called, were expelled from the country. After that scarcely a trace of Arab or Moorish blood remained in the Iberian Peninsula. And very little of their culture either; for apart from the words they had long before brought into the language, the plants and

fruit trees they had introduced, a few skills in pottery and in making *artesonado* ceilings that they passed on to their successors, and a few noble buildings, they left nothing behind them. Even the art of flamenco singing and dancing, which is often thought to be Moorish, owes nothing to them. Their great gift to Europe had been the philosophy and science they had passed on, not to the Spaniards, but to the nations of the north. Even this had not been very original, for the talent of the Arabs in these matters lay in assimilation rather than in original creation, which was reserved for poetry and architecture and for their exquisite materials and handicrafts. But races must be judged for themselves, not for what they convey to others; and so we may be glad that during the darkest age of Western history the Arabs gave to a little corner of Europe a brilliant civilization.

Gerald Brenan is an English writer who has lived in Spain for many years, and whose widely read books about that country include The Spanish Labyrinth *and* South from Granada.

Granada was the last Moslem state in Spain, resisting Christian pressure for two and a half centuries during which it enjoyed an autumnal revival in the arts and commerce (the Alhambra is the chief monument of this period). But in 1492 it was surrendered to Ferdinand and Isabella by Boabdil el Chico (left), who reportedly handed over the keys of the city with the words: "These keys are the last relics of the Arabian empire in Spain. . . . Such is the will of God!" All this is commemorated by a bronze relief in the cathedral showing Boabdil proffering the keys (near left) and the new rulers entering the city (far left).

Opposite: As they were leaving Granada, Boabdil and his party turned back for a last glimpse of the square crenelated towers of the Alhambra. The moment was re-created five centuries later by Washington Irving, who wrote: "The Moorish cavaliers gazed with a silent agony of tenderness and grief upon that delicious abode, the scene of their loves and pleasures. . . . Presently a peal of artillery, faintly heard, told that the city was taken possession of, and the throne of the Moslem kings was lost forever." The height where Boabdil paused to look back has been called ever since El Ultimo Suspiro del Moro, "the last sigh of the Moor."

92

CHILD OF THE FAR FRONTIER

In the wind and weather of the Plains a future

novelist found the source of history's never-failing renewal

By WALLACE STEGNER

Unless everything in a man's memory of childhood is misleading, there is a time somewhere between the ages of five and twelve that corresponds to the phase ethologists have isolated in the development of birds, when an impression lasting only a few seconds may be imprinted on the young bird for life. Expose a just-hatched duckling to an alarm clock, or a wooden decoy on rollers, or a man, or any other object that moves and makes a noise, and it will react to that object for life as if it were its mother. Expose a child to a particular environment at his susceptible time and he will perceive in the shapes of that environment until he dies.

The smell of the gray-leafed shrub called wolf willow brings back my childhood as infallibly as if it were Proust's tea, but other things than smells will do it. I can sing an old Presbyterian Sunday-school hymn, "The Fight Is On, Oh Christian Soldiers," and instantly I am seven or eight years old, it is a June day on the old Saskatchewan homestead, the coulee is full of buttercups, and a flickertail's close-eared head is emerging in jerks from a burrow, the unblinking almond eye watching to see if I move. Only because I must have sung it to myself in that spot, a few bars of that tune can immerse me in the old sun and space, return me to the big geometry of the prairie and the tension of the prairie wind.

I still sometimes dream, occasionally in the most intense and brilliant shades of green, of a jungly dead bend of the Whitemud River below Martin's dam. Each time I am haunted, on awaking, by a sense of meanings just withheld, and by a profound nostalgic melancholy. Yet why should this dead loop of river, known only for a few years, be so charged with potency in my unconscious? Why should there be around it so many other images that constantly recur in dreams or in the phrases I bring up off the typewriter onto the page? They lie in me like underground water; every well I put down taps them.

I suppose I know, actually, why that river dream is so potent. As the summer prairie of the homestead taught me identity by exposing me, the Whitemud River valley where we wintered taught me about safety. In a jumpy and insecure childhood where all masculine elements are painful or dangerous, sanctuary matters. That sunken bottom sheltered from the total sky and the untrammeled wind was my hibernating ground, my place of snugness; and in a country often blistered and crisped, green became the color of safety.

I do not mean to indulge in psychological narcissism. There is something else here, a nature-nurture problem of a more general bearing. For the processes of deculturation, isolation, and intellectual schizophrenia that I underwent as a result of being brought up on a belated, almost symbolic frontier were until recently a most common American experience. Like other Americans uncertain of who they are, I take a firm hold on the certainties of where I am from. I can say to myself that a good part of my private and social

character, the kinds of scenery and weather and people and humor I respond to, the prejudices I wear like dishonorable scars, the affections that sometimes waken me from middle-aged sleep with a rush of undiminished love, the virtues I respect and the weaknesses I condemn, the code I try to live by, the special ways I fail at it and the kinds of shame I feel when I do, the models and heroes I follow, the colors and shapes that evoke my deepest pleasure, the way I adjudicate between personal desire and personal responsibility, have been in good part scored into me by that little womb-village and the lovely, lonely, exposed prairie of the homestead.

However anachronistic I may be, I am a product of the American earth, and in nothing quite so much as in the contrast between what I knew through the pores and what I was officially taught. For education tried, inadequately and hopelessly, against all odds, to make a European of me. I was charged with getting in a single lifetime, from scratch, what some people inherit as naturally as they breathe air. And not merely cultural matters. I was nearly twelve before I saw either a bathtub or a water closet; and when I walked past my first lawn, in Great Falls, Montana, I stooped down and touched its cool nap in awe and unbelief. I think I held my breath—I had not known that people anywhere lived with such grace. Also I had not known until then how much ugliness I myself had lived with. Our homestead yard was as bare as an alkali flat, because my father, observing some folklore fire precaution, insisted on throwing out the soapy wash water until he had killed off every blade of grass or cluster of false mallow inside the fireguard.

Still, there are some advantages to growing up a savage, and to tell the truth I am not sure I would trade my childhood of freedom and the outdoors and the senses for a childhood of being led by the hand past all the Turners in the National Gallery. Anyone starting from deprivation is spared getting bored. You may not get a good start, but you may get up a considerable head of steam. I am reminded of Willa Cather, that bright girl from Nebraska who memorized long passages from the *Aeneid* and hunted down whatever Old World culture was available to her in Red Cloud or Lincoln. She tried, and her education encouraged her, to be a good European. And yet she was a first-rate novelist only when she dealt with what she knew from Red Cloud and the big grasslands. They were what she was born to write; the rest of it was got up. Eventually, when education had won and nurture had conquered nature and she had recognized Red Cloud as a vulgar little hole, she embraced totally the traditions of strangers, and ended neither quite a good American nor quite a true European nor quite a whole artist.

Her career is a parable. If there is truth in D. H. Lawrence's assertion that America's unconscious wish has always been to destroy Europe, there is equal truth in the assertion that every American is an incipient expatriate tempted toward apostasy and reconciliation with the Old World parent. It is a painful division, and the farther you are from Europe—that is, the farther you are out in the hinterlands of America—the more painful it is. Contradictory voices tell you who you are and who you ought to be. You grow up speaking one dialect and reading and writing another. During twenty-odd years of education and another thirty of literary practice you may learn to be nimble in the King's English; yet in moments of relaxation, crisis, or surprise you fall back into the corrupted lingo that is your native tongue. But you can hardly write that lingo if you try: all the forces of Culture and snobbery are against your *writing* by ear, for your most native audience. For one thing, your most native audience doesn't read—it *isn't* an audience. You grow out of touch with your dialect because education and association lead the other way. Only an occasional Mark Twain or Robert Frost speaks with the country tongue. The deculturation of the frontier leads not on to something new but back to an indifferent copy of the abandoned old.

In practice, frontier deculturation means a falling-back on mainly oral traditions, on the things that can be communicated without books: on folklore, on the music and poetry and story easily memorized, on the cookery that comes not from cookbooks but from habit and laziness, on the medicine that is old wives' tales. Before it was more than half assembled from its random parts, the folklore of Whitemud was mine. But I also read whatever books I could lay hands on, and almost everything I got from books was at odds with what I knew from experience or irrelevant to it or remote from it.

Our house contained some novels, mainly by George Barr McCutcheon and Gene Stratton Porter, a set of Shakespeare in marbled bindings with red leather spines and corners, and a massive set of Ridpath's *History of the World*. I handled them all, and I suppose read in them some, uncomprehendingly, from the time I was five. It was my mother's inaccurate boast that I had read clear through Ridpath's eight or nine volumes by the time I was eight.

Let us say that I had looked at the pictures, and learned a few names, and could parrot a few captions. Much of that random rubbish is still in my head like an impression in wax, and comes out of me now as if memory were a phonograph record. What strikes me about this in recollection is not my precocious or fictitious reading capacity, and not the durability of memory, but the fact that the information I was gaining had not the slightest relevance to the geography, history, or life of the place where I lived. Living in the Cypress Hills, I did not even know I lived there, and hadn't the faintest notion of who had lived there before me. But I could have drawn you a crudely approximate map of the Baltic or the Mediterranean, recited you Tom Moore songs or Joaquin Miller's poem about Columbus, and given you a rudimentary notion of the virtues of the Gracchi or the misfortunes of the Sabine women.

Though my friends and I sometimes planned gaudy canoe expeditions down the Whitemud, we had no notion where such a trip might bring us out, and no notion that there were maps which would tell us. The willow-fringed stream, after it left the Hills, might as well have been on its way to join the Alpheus. The Hills of which I was an unknowing resident were only a few fixed points: North Bench, South Bench, the sandhills, Chimney Coulee. I did not relate them, for knowledge of place, like knowledge of the past, meant to me something far and foreign.

In general the assumption of all of us, child or adult, was that this was a new country and that a new country had no history. History was something that applied to other places. It would not have seemed reasonable to any of the town's founders to consider their activities history, or to look back very far in search of what had preceded them. Time reached back only a few years, to the pre-homestead period of the big cattle ranches. Some ranches had weathered the terrible winter of 1906, and to a child these survivors seemed to have been there forever, floating in an enduring present like the town. For that matter, I never heard of the terrible winter of 1906 until many years later, though it had affected my life for me before I was born.

Under the circumstances it might sound fanciful to suggest that either the geography or the history of the Cypress Hills could have had any substantial part in making the minds and characters of children reared there. Certainly they could have no strong and immediate effect, as they might have upon a child who passes every day the rude bridge where the embattled farmers of Concord precipitated a new age with a volley of musketry; or upon a child who flies his kite in the Saratoga meadow where the bronze boot commemorates the nameless heroism of a traitor. The past becomes a thing made palpable in monuments, buildings, historical sites, museums, attics, old trunks, relics of a hundred kinds; and in the legends of grandfathers and great-grandfathers; and in the incised marble and granite and weathered wood of graveyards; and in the murmurings of ghosts. We knew no such history, no such past, no such tradition, no such ghosts. And yet it would be a double error to assume that my childhood had no history, and that I was not influenced by it.

For history is a pontoon bridge. Every man walks and works at its building end, and has come as far as he has over the pontoons laid by others he may never have heard of. Events have a way of making other events inevitable; the actions of men are consecutive and indivisible. The history of the Cypress Hills had almost as definite effects on me as did their geography and weather, though I never knew a scrap of that history until a quarter century after I left the place. However it may have seemed to the people who founded it in 1914, Whitemud was not a beginning, not a new thing, but a stage in a long historical process.

History? Seldom, anywhere, have historical changes occurred so fast. From grizzlies, buffaloes, and Indians still only half-possessed of the horse and gun, the historical parabola to Dust Bowl and near depopulation covered only about sixty years. Here was the Plains frontier in a capsule, condensed into the life of a reasonably long-lived man.

And even though unwritten, it is not lost. Experience enlarges and illuminates it, it continues as remembered faces, it echoes in the head in half-forgotten names, it exists as a part of folklore. Without having been taught, it is to some degree understood. Like the sensuous images persistent from childhood, like the ineradicable attitudes and prejudices, the history of one's truly native place may be comprehended in the bone and the blood, and one may build a life forward from it as surely as if his past had been learned under savants and memorialized in monuments and ruins.

Professor of English at Stanford, Wallace Stegner is also well known as a novelist and historian. This essay will form a part of his new book Wolf Willow, *to be published next month by Viking.*

Nolan's paintings fall into four major groups, the first of which deals with the effects of Australia's capriciously cruel environment. Though a skeleton hanging in a tree may seem far-fetched, Ram Caught in Flood *is in fact based on one of Nolan's own photographs.*

Artist
from
the
Outback

Sidney Nolan

Out of the themes of drought and disaster, the arrogant bravery of an outlaw, and the heroism of his countrymen at Gallipoli, the Australian painter Sidney Nolan is creating a mythology for his native land

There has been no great explosion of the arts in Australia. Since Melba's clear and beautiful voice first emerged out of the cockney twang in the 1890's, the country has had to wait half a century for a soprano with the talents of Joan Sutherland. The best of Australian writers, such as Henry Lawson and Henry Handel Richardson, have hardly risen to the first flight. Neither sculpture nor architecture found much support in a young colony struggling for survival, and the theatre for the most part has relied on importations from abroad. A school of naturalistic landscape painters was at work in the early years of this century, and some, like Penleigh Boyd, achieved distinction, but that was all.

None of this is to be greatly wondered at: after all, the first white settlers arrived in the country barely a century and a half ago; they had to struggle for existence in a wilderness; and even now the entire population hardly exceeds that of New York City. In a good climate the enjoyment of sport, rather than art, was the natural course of things. Australia's record, in short, has been rather like that of the Middle West, a region it much resembles.

Soon after the Second World War, however, it became apparent that a fresh wind was blowing. A group of young novelists appeared, presently a good play came along—Ray Lawler's *The Summer of the Seventeenth Doll*—and a new generation of poets began to look for something beyond the bush ballads that had once been the mainspring of Australian poetry. In painting there was an especially interesting de-

velopment: the work of men like George Russell Drysdale and William Dobell had a detachment that was a decided break from the imitative canvases of the past. And with the emergence of Sidney Nolan it seems possible that Australian painting has achieved a definite emancipation.

Nolan, despite all evidence to the contrary, is an Australian of the Australians. He has evoked his talent in harmony with the peculiar environment of the country. Factory worker, farm hand, cook, sign painter, odd-jobman—he has been all these things. He knows poverty and the crowded back streets of new cities as well as the immense horizons of the outback. The descendant of Irish immigrants, none of whom had any connection with art, Nolan was born in 1917 in the working-class district of Carlton, in Melbourne, and grew up in the shadow of the financial depression, which was particularly hard on a new country where hardly anyone had resources of any kind. He left school at the age of fifteen and took jobs where he could find them. Painting—he began to attend life classes before he was sixteen—reading, and the writing of poetry (he has been almost as much poet as painter at times) were preoccupations that had to be pursued on the side and often at night. All this is typical of the struggle every sensitive and intelligent Australian boy had in a materialistic environment that turned to beer, betting, and sport for relaxation and rejected as "soft" and probably bogus any pretensions to culture or art.

But the essence of Nolan's Australian-ness goes a good

By ALAN MOOREHEAD

Taken from the artist's sequence on the austere Australian outback, Camel Buggy *captures the essence of that inhospitable landscape, with its vacant horizon uninterrupted by any traveler.*

deal deeper than this, for he possesses to the full that sense of nostalgia, of bereftness, of isolation, which up to now has been at the root of the Australian approach to life. The paintings on these pages are, to some extent, Nolan's expression of that incompleteness; and in expressing it, he conquers it.

Let me be a little more explicit. Australians of my generation grew up in a world apart. Until we went abroad we had never seen a beautiful building, hardly ever heard a foreign language spoken or been to a well-acted play, or eaten a reasonably sophisticated meal, or listened to a good orchestra; and outside the two or three art galleries in Melbourne and Sydney there was scarcely a house that contained a collection of worthwhile paintings. Nor were any of these matters much talked about. This was not absolutely a cultural vacuum, for we had books (Australians per head are the greatest readers in the world), magazines, Gramophone records, prints and, on another level, the movies and the radio. The trouble with all these things was that they were importations, reproductions which were only an image of the originals. And inevitably any strivings that we ourselves made toward the intellectual and artistic life were, very largely, an imitation of these importations from abroad. Australian women dressed themselves according to European

fashions; and the well-to-do man's first thought was to make a trip abroad—to return for a visit to the British Isles, the home of his ancestors and the center of the full, rich, and stimulating life that we imagined went on in the outer world.

Even the very animals we bred were dependent upon periodical return to Europe, for it was soon discovered that horses, cattle, and other stock (though not sheep) declined after the third generation unless they were refreshed by new blood brought in from England and Ireland. Australia, apart from its gold and its eucalyptus and wattle trees, seemed to contribute nothing of its own.

There was another aspect of our isolation that was less consciously felt but was just as important. We had no history, no past behind us. No invasion or civil war had uprooted Australia during its brief history—the wars were all abroad—and with the exception of the aborigines, no one had ever lived in the country before us. There were no ruins, no relics of past civilizations, no myths, no reassuring sense of the continuity of things.

After the first exploration of the country the best we could do in the way of local history was a miners' disturbance known as the Eureka Stockade, and the adventures of a young Irish desperado named Ned Kelly. Kelly was a bushranger, a highwayman who robbed banks and pubs in

An uncanny mood of melancholy is evoked by the perversely up-side-down bird in Feeding the Birds, *among Nolan's early paintings.*

country towns, and he made his last stand against the police in an iron-pipelike helmet with a slit in it for his eyes. We rather liked Ned Kelly. We felt he expressed some of our own freebooting irritation with authority, our own tough approach to life. We thought we had to be tough, I suspect, partly because we wanted to disguise our inner loneliness.

Nolan, so far as I can see, is bedeviled by none of these misgivings, and this is a fundamental aspect of his work. He accepts the world in which he grew up, he sees the Australian predicament, and it does not distress or embarrass him. Instead he makes a virtue of it. He discovers beauty and myth in places where hardly anyone had looked before; he realizes that no one is really isolated and that the Australian scene is merely a re-creation of the ancient past. A myth, a continuous dream, explains and animates the human race, and the same hates and loves are with us all the time. It is to the painting of that dream that Nolan, with a peculiar concentration and originality—for he imitates no other painter I can think of—has devoted his life.

Success—and by success I also mean that sense of fulfillment a creative man has when he knows that he is on the right track and working to the limit of his powers—did not come to him at all easily. From his earliest student days he has never been conventional. His subjects at first were ab-

stract, and his first one-man show was a collection of calligraphic fantasies and collages. One outraged visitor threw a pot of green paint at the exhibits. Nolan has never painted on canvas but chooses instead a coated and glazed paperboard, glass, or Masonite, and pigments of his own invention, such as an admixture of poster paints and polyvinyl acetate. Even later on, when he turned to studies with a recognizable subject, his paintings were still a long way from what most people thought a painting ought to be. Not surprisingly it has only been within the past few years that there has been any widespread appreciation or knowledge of the great force and truth of his originality.

Nolan is an artist who works in a state of continuous experiment, and he is constantly returning to old themes in the midst of discovering new ones. Nevertheless there appear to have been, up to date, four main subjects in his painting, and one of the earliest of these was concerned with the droughts that descend on the Australian outback from time to time. Natural disasters—bush fires, floods, and drought—played a great part in our national consciousness in Australia. In a young country, where we had no reserves either of man power or money, it was an annihilating thing to see your wooden house burned down, your crops swept away by a cloudburst, and your animals die for the lack of grass.

Nolan is probably best known for Kelly, *from his series on the famous outlaw of that name. Here a sleight-of-hand perspective makes him resemble a centaur, the classic image of a lawless, barbaric hero.*

Drought caused the worst havoc. It was a slow and paralyzing business, the sun beating down week after week from a brassy sky, the land turning from green to lifeless brown, the cattle with their protruding ribs, standing listlessly on the open plain; and there was nothing, absolutely nothing, that could be done about it. The stockrider, with bitterness, grew accustomed to the sight of the white bones of his dead cattle scattered around the dried-up water hole. This was death in an immensity of space, a ruthless and natural inevitability. But there remained, as Nolan discovered in his drawings, a marvelous abstraction in the skeleton lying on the sand, a suggestion that death, though terrible, was by no means a vile or an ugly thing. There is a mute nobility in the simple pattern of its bones.

About Ned Kelly I am not quite so sure. One descends here from the general disaster to the particular tragedy, from the natural abstraction to the human myth. As bushrangers go, young Kelly (he was only twenty-five when he was finally caught and executed) was a cut above his kind. He made war upon the government rather than upon individuals, and the letter in which he explained his motives to the world is the eloquent and convinced plea of a revolutionary rather than a criminal. Yet a criminal he was; there was no place for him in a settled community, and if we are

to consider him sympathetically, we must do so on his own terms: as a brave and unrepentant misfit, as the avenger of injustice, as one man defying destiny, as the personification of the poet's idea that an hour of glorious life is worth an age without a name. This I think is Nolan's approach to the Kelly saga. He is on Kelly's side. His haunting, monolithic figure in the iron mask has the flames of hell upon it, but that slit for the eyes is wonderfully expressive of defiance: this is the crisis of the strong man in chaos, and once again the tragedy is beautiful. With his Kelly paintings Nolan began to reach up toward the full range of his special talent, the uninhibited expression of an emotion in paint.

The Leda and the Swan sequence that followed has a much wider, freer, and surer scope, and the pictures represent a temporary departure from the Australian scene. They are the result of Nolan's having left Australia for the first time, in 1950, and of his having lived for a while, after many travels, on the Greek island of Hydra. We have swans in Australia, black ones as well as white; the stark rocks and the limpid sunshine of the Aegean are not unlike some of our more arid coasts in the south; and the notion of the lover eagerly received is a universal thing—but that is about as far as the Australian connection goes in these lyrical, half-erotic fantasies of the yearning woman waiting alone

Ned Kelly was finally captured, with 28 bullet wounds in his body, at the hotel in Glenrowan. Kelly at Glenrowan, *showing the splintered hotel walls, the shattered armor, and still defiant figure of the lone bushranger, commemorates this last chapter in his legend.*

The theme of Leda and the Swan appears in Landscape, *which also bears the swirling brush marks of Nolan's recent work.*

and the god Zeus descending on wings upon her from the sky. It was the floating, dreamlike ecstasy of Nolan's lovers that made such a sensation when they were first shown in London, and the eerie landscapes gave one the impression that they had been painted by night—as well they might have been. This was a conception of perfect physical love in a wilderness; and his two figures, the twining dominant swan and the woman utterly obsessed, gave it wonderful life and warmth.

The Gallipoli paintings, Nolan's fourth phase and possibly his best work yet, are another matter. Here he returns to an Australian theme, but applies to it the same otherworldly feeling he expressed through Leda and the Swan. The myth here is very strong, for it is recent history. Every boy who grew up in Australia in the first half of this century knew all about Gallipoli. It was the country's first foreign war, the first test of its men in battle. Some tens of thousands of young soldiers were sent to the Gallipoli Peninsula in 1915 to take part in the attempt of the Allies to force the Dardanelles and throw Turkey out of the war. They failed, but they failed magnificently; and today every township in Australia has its Gallipoli monument. Nolan's generation grew up in a world where the older men were forever talking

More than any of Nolan's other paintings, the Gallipoli

102

campaign series (from which The Myth Rider *is taken) embodies his attempt to proclaim an authentically Australian artistic tradition*

about Gallipoli. It was the symbol of the country's courage and of its coming of age, and it was a perfect subject for Nolan: the heroic legend, the young Australian soldier on the classical battlefield of the Hellespont, the linking of the young country with the ancient civilization of Greece. He has evoked all this with almost a religious depth of feeling, of dedication, and of poetry—the very emotions with which the soldiers actually fought. His painting of the young light-horseman with the feathers flying from his hat is a classical hero translated to the modern age, and the lonely, ghostly bodies floating on the Aegean shore are part of a universal suffering. The figures of his naked soldiers remind one of the athletes on an Attic vase.

Nolan now lives in London and in the midst of his recent, remarkable success has produced a spate of other work—book jackets, theatre décor, lithographs—so much of it, indeed, that some of his friends have wondered whether his talents might not suffer from too much expression. But he seems to work with extraordinary facility and extraordinary fidelity; and he himself is such a natural, friendly, unaffected man that it is quite unlikely that he will be spoiled by the recognition he is now receiving all over the world.

Unlike most artists he travels a great deal. The Arizona desert and the temples of Angkor, India and Italy, the Middle East and the valley of the Lower Nile, all these and many more have drawn him along a Jason-like journey in search of the golden myth. But it is his Australian background that probably moves him most, however cosmopolitan he may have become. He plans once more to return to the outback to study those parched and desiccated forms on the red earth. He has also been working at the illustration of a long, esoteric poem by the Australian Alwyn Lee. It is a nostalgic work about their mutual birthplace, Melbourne, a filtering-through of early memories to a sophisticated present, somewhat in the manner of James Joyce. After all, Nolan *knows* this world, the pubs and the football crowds, the bush fires and the surf bathers on the Pacific beach; and he was born just in time to have a whiff of the early pioneering days when earthen roads came into the heart of the city and the farmer, returning from market, rode off with his horse and buggy across an endless plain.

In recent years a million immigrants have descended on Australia, atomic piles are being built in the bush, and jet planes are in the sky. The old isolation is over and done with forever. Yet all these changes would be confused and meaningless without a tradition—the continuous racial instinct that reaches out of the past and into the future. Nolan more than any other living artist has observed this tradition and has refreshed and illuminated it by his work.

Alan Moorehead, an Australian who is now living in Italy, last contributed to HORIZON *in September, 1960. One of his many books,* Gallipoli, *provided a part of the stimulus for Sidney Nolan's series of paintings on that tragic campaign.*

We invite you to consider Burgess Hill School

Located on a country estate near London, this coeducational board-
ing school has been offering instruction to talented pupils between
the ages of five and eighteen. The rambling eighteenth-century house
shown above, surrounded by spacious grounds, was acquired only
recently by this unique institution. Burgess Hill was founded
twenty-eight years ago, and dedicated to the most advanced peda-
gogical principles of our day. The philosophy of the school, as
summed up by its Headmaster, is to develop "one's whole personality alongside other people." A staff of sixteen has encouraged the
self-expression of just thirty-six students, many of them the children of artists, architects, and actors. Fees are £106 ($290) per term.
Those wishing further information are requested to turn the page.

...where the student is really free

Seen as on the page before, but here with a wider camera angle, the picturesque approach of this progressive school is marred by a derelict car. House paint is peeling, windows are broken.

A group of Burgess Hill students enjoy a casual smoke, wearing the unofficial school "uniform" of baggy sweaters and blue jeans.

*Concentration on carpentry calls
for a cigarette. Another boy reportedly
prefers a glass of ale during recess.*

*The main room at Burgess Hill is
dominated by the old fireplace, touchingly
littered with mementos, and a
handy place to rest bare feet at teatime.*

"Do-as-you-please," and no nonsense about it, has been the motto of Burgess Hill—a vanguard experiment in modern education, and one literally without rules. Students attend classes or not, as they prefer. They wear what they wish, say what they like, eat and sleep when they choose. The Headmaster, James East (right), a Cambridge graduate and former theology student, has asked only that they obey him on such matters as "not climbing on the roof because the slates keep dropping off."

As a result, the school presents the somewhat disheveled appearance seen in the photographs on this and the opposite page. There is little furniture — mostly wooden benches and tables. Some of the walls are covered by murals, mainly of an abstract persuasion, painted by the art teacher and his pupils; others are simply scribbled on.

An advantage for teachers at Burgess Hill, according to the Headmaster, has been that the students want to learn; otherwise they wouldn't come to classes—but he has admitted that the staff must work hard to hold their attention. Have they worked hard enough? Troubles have beset them. The only real disadvantage of this pioneer venture is that, since these photographs were taken, it has been forced to shut down for lack of funds. "Goodbye," one London newspaper headlined the news, "to a child's utopia."

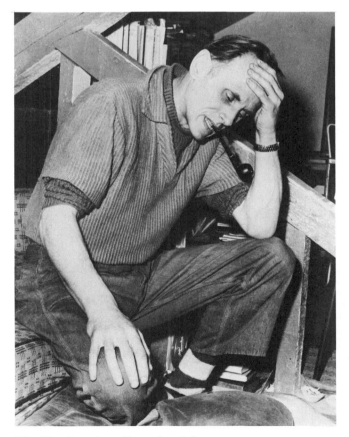

*The Headmaster after a hard day:
"Rules," he has said, "would
make everything rather senseless."
But maybe a little easier?*

MOVIES

The Art of Going it Alone

For the past eight or nine years Morris Engel of New York has been producing his own motion pictures with the assistance of his wife, Ruth Orkin (a leading still photographer in her own right), and a few collaborators. Independent movie-making generally refers to the combination of a group of experts—writers, cameramen, editors—who have broken away from one of the colossi of Hollywood and gone into business for themselves. With a little luck, they may create a new colossus of their own. This does not describe the situation of Engel, whose independence is of a different sort.

What we now call the New Wave originates with him. It was Engel who first went into the streets with a moving-picture camera and photographed whatever moved past the lens, making no attempt to avoid the peripheral activity in the neighborhood or to bring the space about his actors under control. Accidental sounds and motions enter into his pictures as they will. After him have come the French *nouvelle vaguistes*, and an increasing number of low-budget movie makers in New York. In an age that has witnessed the triumph of collective effort, or team spirit, in backward China as in mechanical Detroit, Engel has tried to recover the mobility and adaptability possible only to individuals. It is hard to describe his peculiar virtue. He has grasped the idea that the progress of technology may make large, cumbersome, joint efforts obsolete in films. He has designed his own equipment to give the cameraman flexibility and free him from sets and sound stages, from creation by conference and consultation. As a producer-director—an entrepreneur in his own right—Engel writes scenarios, raises capital (few will envy him that), recruits actors, selects settings, and finally edits his own "rushes." Then, when the films are ready, he still has to go out and find distributors; he proceeds, that is, without prior guarantees from outside producers or distributing organizations. Every art depends for its progress on the courage (and sometimes on the obstinacy) of such innovators. But they cannot expect to have an easy time. Completing a film on one's own is a costly and wearing business; subsequently persuading distributors to "place" it may prove even harder.

Engel has made three full-length pictures, one of which, *The Little Fugitive* (1953), has been shown throughout the United States and widely overseas. Of the two others, *Lovers and Lollipops* (1955) has also been exhibited in this country (though with less financial success than *The Little Fugitive*), and *Weddings and Babies* (1959) had a preview showing at one theatre in New York City but has not been seen elsewhere.

The director gives the reasons for this neglect with great calm and forbearance. The exhibitors are not scoundrels, but their theatres are valuable properties, and they are obliged to run them at a profit. If they are going to exhibit films that depart from the reliable Hollywood pattern, they want them to be money-makers like *La Dolce Vita* or *Never on Sunday*. Not by so much as a murmur did Engel, when I spoke to him, offer to criticize either of these films. He is perhaps more concerned to forge ahead with several new projects of his own.

Starting out as a still photographer, Engel was for many years on the staff of the New York newspaper *PM*, working mainly in the city, occasionally going on distant assignments, covering strikes and murders, but also recording the daily lives of families he lived with for weeks at a time. From journalism he turned to films.

The scene of his movies is New York. Their subject is ordinary life, the life the late Billy de Beck used to describe as "Parlor, Bedroom, and Sink." Engel works in the streets of Manhattan, in West Side and Greenwich Village interiors, on Coney Island, in the harbor, parks, and zoos, and at the top of the Empire State Building.

Lovers and Lollipops, for example, has more city than story in it and strikes the viewer as being a tour of what a social worker might call Community Resources. The photography is superb, and Engel's expert work with the camera—his taste in the choice of lights and angles—provides the main interest of the film and its unity. The images themselves are required to make up for the absence of a story. The visible and the audible are intended to propose fresh, contemporary meanings. The look of a summer street, the appearance of a child in a doorway at night, the rows of cars in the parking lot at

Rockaway Beach—these things demand that we discover for ourselves the principles that connect them.

The honesty of *Lovers and Lollipops* has a certain shock value; we begin to see what a film might be, and how we are treated by conventional movies with their dressed-up and painted figures, spiced and sexualized, placed in expensive and luxurious settings, glamorized on Park Avenue, glamorized in the Far West, and even in the slums and the underworld. To see things as they really are, as we meet them daily, unthinkingly, is curiously startling. It becomes clear at least that what is familiar is in any number of ways made abstract by our avoidance, by the conclusions we refuse to draw from the sight of the well-known sofa, the corner table, the familiar look. We discover the power of the hard and succinct fact, of a woman's face wan with disappointment, of the bristles of a man's beard, or of muffled words and random gestures, of the closeness of summer on the stoop of a brownstone house.

In *Lovers and Lollipops* the interest of the film is almost entirely in the recording of these facts, for the human material is rather poor and bleak, threadbare, lacking depth and shading. The lovers are a widow and a young man home on a holiday from his job in South America. The widow has a little daughter whose feelings, now that a marriage is in prospect, must be given very special consideration. There, in the child, is the *problem*—the problem of psychology, or liberal pedagogy, of patience and decency. The couple worry about her. But she is spirited and impulsive, while they are harassed and wooden. There is, it appears, more sorrow than love between them; the woman is enveloped in a sourceless anxiety or sadness. In an empty new house that she and her young man have gone in a holiday mood to look over, the woman waits alone while her lover goes on a brief errand in a rented car, and for no apparent reason her dread grows. She hears bells and sirens, and fears the worst, yielding to her habitual mood. Hardly anything she does is free from it, and we are afraid for her even when she is laughing, her substance is so meager and her happiness so fragile. To look at ordinary life like this—Engel himself seems to feel, judging by the changes he has made in his more recent work—is rather depressing. One would have to believe fanatically in plain people to think that a formless realism could justify itself by the implicit merit or dignity of plainness. The plainness of plain people is not a thing that is simply thrust on them. They themselves help to achieve it.

If Engel were nothing but an extraordinary cameraman, we would have to say that he had laid out some very sharp instruments but had as yet performed no operation. *The Little Fugitive*, however, the story of a small boy straying on Coney Island—curious, frightened, avid, sad, touching—is a charming film, and *Weddings and Babies* is even better. Engel is not bucking the system merely to be obstinate. He has his own very definite ideas of what a film should be, he is capable of realizing them, and the progress he makes in each successive picture is astonishing. It occurred to me after I had seen only *The Little Fugitive* that he held advanced theoretical notions or prejudices such as flourish in France today among novelists like Robbe-Grillet who dismiss narrative interest altogether and consider character and personality to be based on an obsolete psychology. Because of Engel's photographic passion for things shown literally, I guessed that he had an up-to-date theory of his own. My guess, however, was wrong.

*T*he story of *Weddings and Babies*, Engel's latest picture, which was filmed with portable camera and sound equipment—a novel synchronized sight-and-sound process that was developed by Engel himself—starts off a little lamely, with a woman who wishes to marry the man, and the man, a photographer, resisting naturally enough, pleading that he must support his old mother. The woman, Viveca Lindfors, turns in a stunning performance. The man, John Myhers, is a capable actor. But the anonymous old Italian immigrant who plays the mother breaks through every contrivance of the plot with smashing immediacy. There she is, stout and old, a sinking, squarish frame of old bones, tireless, with hairs on her chin and a toothless mouth, talking to herself in Italian. She is at least partly senile but has enough sense and dignity to be more than merely pitiable. Viveca Lindfors wants to marry and have babies while there is still time. She feels she is cheapening herself in an endless love affair. The photographer wants a new camera to build a sounder future and make something of himself. (Weddings and babies are the mainstay of the dreary trade he wants to get away from, in order to attempt something more important.) The old mother wants shelter (with the aid of Social Security money) and an angel affixed to her tombstone. She escapes from a home for the aged and the care of its nuns to go out to Queens on the subway. In the stonecutter's yard she stops to marvel at the face of the angel. Then she goes to a cemetery not far away. What happens there is as impressive as anything I've ever seen on the screen. News of his mother's disappearance has broken up the birthday party at which the photographer has given Viveca Lindfors an engagement ring (the result, alas, of pressure applied by Viveca). Looking for his mother among the graves, the photographer begins to feel that he cannot give up his freedom and his opportunities to distinguish himself, to be something.

Here we begin to realize more definitely what we have already sensed in earlier frames of the picture: that when the situation is clear, when the feeling is right, Engel can penetrate the hard surfaces of appearance, make the stones eloquent, cause subways and pavements to cry out to us, the millions of dead in clumsily marked rows to influence us. The lesson of the dead, as the photographer reads it, is that he must act before it is too late. He must fulfill himself before he is overtaken by the grave. A bit of psychiatry now creeps in to dim the effect of the great city cemetery. Viveca pronounces her lover not yet free from Mama and walks off. But at film's end the photographer, alone in his melancholy and empty studio, is dialing his Viveca on the telephone, and the signs are that he will recover her. No other resolution seems possible. In the face of old age and death, weddings are still performed and brides hunger for children.

Morris Engel, going it alone, is proving that the quality of a picture filmed independently is different from the results of collective effort. A large team must inevitably have a leveling effect on the imagination of any single member of it. Besides, there is the pressure of money. The thought of several million dollars invested in a film is enough to change the giddy artist into a sober bureaucrat. Engel seems to be asking whether there is not some way to free the film maker from the complexities of organization and the power of the dollar.   SAUL BELLOW

THEATRE

On Being Upstaged by Scenery

The theatre in the 1960's is the heir to so many inventions and traditions of stage design—expressionism, constructivism, the box set, the unit set, the apron stage, theatre-in-the-round, Reinhardt's flyspecks, Gordon Craig's screens, Adolphe Appia's expectant emptiness—that any orderly review of their evolution and intertwined influence is a task for the historian, not the essayist. But it has been, speaking very broadly, a two-edged inheritance. We are the beneficiaries of the Greek amphitheatre and Shakespeare's "Wooden O"; we have also incurred a guilty knowledge of those architectural splendors and natural stupefactions (Vesuvius in spate, the

great seas in uproar) that in centuries past threatened to efface the drama in the cause of spectacle. True, it has been a generation or more since Eliza skipped across the tumbling ice; large and exotic animals are at present out of stage-fashion; and I cannot remember the last time a performer made his entrance upon a cloud. Still, the temptation to confuse the magic of the theatre with the trickery of the stage is in our blood, and our sets today fall roughly into two categories: they offer a picture or they offer a playing space.

Obviously, these alternatives are almost never presented in pure form—the most picture-oriented set must still provide the actors with the physical essentials of their trade, and only the most dedicated theorist will sweep his stage as naked as a laboratory table. Nevertheless, you can usually tell whether the stage was set primarily to flatter the eye or to facilitate the actor's assignment. I can illustrate the difference by describing an experiment that was unaccountably abandoned in 1957 at the Shakespeare Festival in Stratford, Connecticut.

The Stratford theatre, a remote descendent of Shakespeare's Globe, is a house of inviting proportions, admirable acoustics, and great technical versatility. But its stage is vast in all its dimensions, and sets scaled to fill it place the action in jeopardy. I well remember the dress rehearsal of *Julius Caesar* in 1955, the company's first season, when shortly after midnight it was decided to scrap Horace Armistead's breathtaking panorama of Rome because it was diminishing the affairs of Cassius and Brutus to triviality.

For the second season, Rouben Ter-Arutunian designed a stage that seemed to me an ideal frame for Shakespeare. It consisted of tremendous panels of lattice, walling the entire playing area; neutral in tone, these took light and shadow beautifully. Moreover, they were infinitely flexible: openings could be made almost at will; sections could be thrust forward to provide balconies, rostrums, battlements; inner stages, dungeons, grottoes, private doors, or ceremonial gateways could be conjured out of the pliant slatwork. Since the lattice was ambiguous—interior or exterior, nature or fabrication—any object added to it was vividly suggestive, and a very few props—a tapestry, a throne chair, stacked arms, a glowing brazier—would sharply focus the scene. The space was as great as ever, but it was space undefined by perspective or scale, and in that limpid element the actors took on the heightened presence that is part of what makes theatre magic. I don't know why the Shakespeare Festival shelved this exemplary scene for the pastel and papier-mâché agitation that became its style in later seasons. This theatre does business primarily with the summer colonies along the shore; perhaps such an audience does not appreciate self-effacement raised to an art.

The question of whether the stage is to be a vision or an instrument is linked to equivalent theories as to the relationship between the audience and the occasion; it has been given particular relevance in our time by the proliferation of theatres in accommodations never meant for the drama. If the playwright is the manufacturer of more or less intelligent pastimes for a market that can pay well to be amused, then everything possible should be done to present a beguiling package. I have considerable admiration for the professional efficiency of *A Man for All Seasons*, but it falls, I think, into the category of entertainment. And its eye-catching unit set, dominated by a magnificently proportioned spiral ramp, its scene changes wittily engineered into the action, suit the intentions of the work and contribute to its popular success.

Such decorative virtuosity, however, makes an almost tangible barrier of the proscenium frame; the audience feels itself in exile from fairyland. I recall still the elegant sensuality of Christian Bérard's set for the production of *L'Ecole des Femmes*, which Louis Jouvet brought to America a good many years ago. The insolently aristocratic chandeliers, the exquisitely scaled street arches, the garden walls that parted on silken hinges to disclose the most perfect of formal gardens—these blandishments of texture and proportion made the audience purr. But I also remember that I watched Molière through flawless plate glass: one looked in rapture, but one was not touched.

The playgoer who forsakes such luxury of the senses for the opportunism of off-Broadway may feel himself curtly received, unless at the same time he shifts his view of himself from pampered guest to committed participant. No one perched on the bleachers of the 4th Street Theatre—that railroad flat bisected by a card-table stage —deluded himself that the theatre is a spectator sport. If a play took life in those surroundings, it was because audience and cast willed that it should do so; and perhaps because the challenge was so obvious, the miracle occurred there with dependable regularity. I don't pretend that this former American home of Chekhov and Ibsen was ideal for its purposes: I was disconcerted by spying a second audience, a kind of mirror image, dimly across the lighted playing area; the little stage was so crabbed that one ground plan had to be used, play after play.*

The off-Broadway definition of a theatre is any room that can seat one hundred or more persons without incurring the instant hostility of the fire department. Sometimes these unlikely warrens are brilliantly suited to the material at hand. José Quintero's production of *The Iceman Cometh* at the original Circle in the Square (it has

*Mr. Ross has now left the 4th Street Theatre for a church in the West Fifties, which is being remodeled and should open as a theatre this fall.

since been torn down to make way for an apartment house) fitted with almost no artifice at all into the long, bleak room, broken by pillars supporting the low ceiling. And the Provincetown Playhouse, mean in dimensions, grimy, threadbare, neglected, was a den ready-made for Krapp's prowlings. I recall, finally, the throat-constricting expectancy of that operating table of a stage deep below the tiered seats where *The Blacks* was played. It was made a place of ritual merely by the vertiginous pitch of its sight lines.

There are evident limitations to the lucky compatibility between house and play. These absurd theatres of Greenwich Village and the East Side have proved excellent frames for the Theatre of the Absurd that now dominates our avant-garde; but their idiosyncracies and raffish squalor do not always suit: Congreve's *The Way of the World* stepped its minuet bravely at The Cherry Lane, but it seemed to be slumming. Despite an almost continual ululation in the profession, poverty can be a tonic in the theatre, but I would not therefore prescribe it as the principal diet.

What is so inspiriting about these makeshift stages, however, is that the room for a play often seems to have been created by main force. The audience feels itself a crowd of witnesses on the verge of trespassing upon the minimal arena where the performers are getting on with their imperative task. At The Living Theatre it has become almost a matter of style that the actors exhort patrons to join the act. The revivalist appeal is hardly necessary, for the house itself throws everyone into the melee.

*U*ptown in the more decorous houses, formalized by their curtains and proscenium stages, it is not as easy to mount a performance that takes on the quality of a communal ceremony. Nevertheless, the distinction between picture-scape and playing space still operates. A set, when it is first revealed, should make you inch forward in your seat; too often, it urges you to lean back after perfunctory applause. The designers, members of one of the few real guilds left in the world, work with such authority, so fill the stage with their strong personalities, that there often seems no opening for author or actors. Tennessee Williams's *The Night of the Iguana* is a case in point. The play impressed me as the most relevant, most humane, dramatically most engrossing work that Williams has done in some time. But I was aware that the playwright was fighting the set for my attention. This fully conceived hotel of dubious propriety, deep in the Mexican jungle, projected so much personality of its own, its cunning angles and subtle imbalances were so diverting, its vegetation so feverishly rich, that the cross purposes, precarious sanity, and rampant vitality of the play's personnel were gentled by the visual boisterousness. The performances, though good, were perhaps a little too consistently strident. That could be accounted for by the presence of Bette Davis, whose professional aura does not encourage reticence in her colleagues, but the steaming jungle must take a share of the blame.

I dislike a set that stands on its own feet: it should be like a bicycle—functional only in motion. Thus the sets for *Ross*, a play I did not much admire, seemed to me excellent. They were so shallow, sometimes so perfunctory, as to be disagreeably saltless in repose. But they keyed the action and stood well aside to let the actors get everything humanly possible out of the script. Of course *Ross* is a play in innumerable scenes, and the budget for individual tableaux must have been spartan. A writer these days who constructs a one-set play invites the designer to paint him off the stage.

Box sets are out of favor just now, but they have a great virtue: they allow the performance to build emotion under the pressure of confinement. Still, the emphasis of these boxes should be on the space they enclose and not on the furnishings the designer can plausibly pack them with to "heighten" the illusion. Nothing so deflates illusion as bric-a-brac that upstages the actor. Such sets invariably draw applause as the curtain rises on a parlormaid dusting the armor; in my view, any set that draws applause should instantly be scrapped for a plain backdrop. Stage design is like editing or undertaking—no trade for prima donnas.

I say that, realizing that the two greatest figures of modern stage design—Adolphe Appia and Gordon Craig—were prima donnas of the first rank. But they were also seers, men transfixed by all-embracing visions. Appia decreed a stage of neutral emptiness to be transformed by light; Craig appealed to the theatre world to be saved by his "thousand scenes in one scene"—a distillation of the total human environment which, translated, became: "flat floor—flat walls—flat roof." The stage structures imagined by these men were noble, expectant, almost religious, and fairly crying out for great deeds and inexorable decisions. But in both cases they also bore a strong resemblance to Stonehenge or the Giant's Causeway; had they prevailed, they could have restricted the repertory to Wagner, *King Lear*, and Ibsen's *When We Dead Awaken*.

However, the theatre has never been in danger of succumbing to the high-minded rigors of Craig and Appia. The kind of threat it does have to be on guard against is the staircase that is more beautiful than the heroine, the living room that is busier than the villain, and the forest of Arden in which you cannot see Touchstone for the trees.   ROBERT HATCH

BOOKS

History by Another Name

The brothers Goncourt, Edmond and Jules, were nobly born. They were rich. But they had the misfortune to be intelligent. Therefore they were unhappy. They wanted to be famous; they longed to be eminent authors, princes in the realm of literature; they yearned for immortality. Together, they wrote novels and plays which made a certain impression in their time but which are now forgotten, surviving only on library shelves and in courses on nineteenth-century French literature. In spite of all their efforts and aspirations, they died unsatisfied and sad: Jules of syphilis in 1870, Edmond of old age in 1896.

But before they died, they designed their monuments: a record and an institution.

The institution was the Académie Goncourt. This was a piece of monumental snobbery. Jules and Edmond had failed to be elected to *the* Academy, the Académie Française, in whose forty chairs sit the gold-braided peers, saints, and guardians of French Culture. Therefore they created an Academy of their own, which still exists. In imitation of its founders it does no hard, regular work, but confers magisterial awards of approbation and money upon French authors—some of whom have been a good deal more eloquent and imaginative than Jules and Edmond but who, like warriors kneeling before a palsied *roi fainéant*, feel that they have really achieved a new distinction.

The record was the Goncourt *Journal*, that remarkable literary document which was published only a few years ago in its entirety, and of which we now have a selection in English, translated and edited with a good introduction by Robert Baldick (*Pages from the Goncourt Journal;* Oxford University Press). As soon as the brothers started to go out together into literary circles and into "society," they began to keep a joint daybook, recording conversations and gossip, criticizing new plays, estimating new personalities. It is a vivid and pungent piece of writing and an unforgettable thing to read. They began it together in 1851, with a horribly elaborate sentence as an overture. (In December of that year Louis Napoleon Bonaparte, duly elected President of the French Republic, had just arrested the leaders of the chief political parties, dismissed the legislature, and made himself dictator: this event was the subject of their first paragraph.*) Together they kept their diary for nearly twenty years: Jules did most of the actual writing, but both supplied the material and shaped the phrases. Even after Jules died, the chain of habit was too strong to break, and Edmond continued the journal alone, keeping it faithfully until his death. In his later years he issued nine volumes of extracts from it, which were very ill received: few of his acquaintances enjoyed having their indiscretions recorded and repeated and their characters dissected with a red-hot scalpel. The entire journal, whose manuscript was preserved in the French National Library, did not appear until more than a century after it was begun.

The four hundred pages of Robert Baldick's selection cover more than forty years of French social, political, and aesthetic history. France had great men in numbers in those days, and the Goncourts knew most of them. Hugo, Zola, Rodin, Degas, Renan, Sainte-Beuve, Flaubert, Dumas *père* and *fils*, all these and many others either appear in person or are heard off stage. The chief value of the *Journal* comes from the Goncourts' gift for gathering and recording vivid impressions, illuminating anecdotes, evanescent sights, and winged words. Thus:

In the sombre winter of 1870, Victor Hugo spoke the obituary of Napoleon III's regime: "The Empire did nothing to provide a defense against foreigners; everything it did was designed to provide a defense against the population."

Flaubert told the story of a man who was taken fishing by a friend. The friend was an atheist. They fished up a stone on which was carved: I DO NOT EXIST. *Signed:* GOD. "There!" said the atheist. "What did I tell you?"

Oscar Wilde told Henri de Régnier, "I've been married three times in my life, once to a woman and twice to men."

Discussing the dangers of exaggerated realism on the stage, Daudet told of a woman in deep mourning who boarded a bus. She looked so tragically unhappy that a neighbor asked her for the story of her misfortunes. With the passengers murmuring their sympathy and the conductor blowing his nose to hide his tears, she de-

scribed the death of her first child, then the death of her second. But by the time she got to the death of her third child, interest began to slacken; and when she narrated the death of her fourth child, which was eaten alive by a crocodile on the banks of the Nile, everyone burst out laughing.

Besides many such anecdotes, there are some rapidly sketched but memorable scenes. The Goncourts would have made fine reporters. Thus:

Maupassant rushing into the water at Etretat to save a drowning man who was quite drunk: he turned out to be Swinburne.

A group of Communist prisoners being taken to execution after their failure to seize Paris. "Among the women, one was singularly beautiful, with the implacable beauty of a young Fate. She was a girl with dark curly hair, steely eyes, and cheekbones red with dried tears. She stood frozen as it were in a defiant posture, hurling insults at officers and men from a throat and lips so contracted by anger that they were unable to form words. 'She's just like the girl who stabbed Barbier!' a young officer said to one of his friends."

In December, 1870, Edmond Goncourt visited a butcher's shop that (because Paris was blockaded) had bought some of the animals from the zoo. "On the wall, hung in a place of honor, was the skinned trunk of the elephant . . . and a boy was offering some camel's kidneys for sale. . . . I fell back on a couple of larks which I carried off for my lunch."

*A*nd, since this is a French book, there are some cutting epigrams: "Any picture that produces a moral impression is a bad picture. . . . There are very few cases of bereavement in which the woman does not say: 'It's a good thing I didn't buy a summer dress.' . . . Renan's brain was like a deconsecrated cathedral, full of piles of wood, bales of straw, and heaps of assorted lumber, but retaining its religious architecture."

The best way to appreciate the Goncourt *Journal* is to see it not as a collection of miscellaneous and fragmentary paragraphs but as a kind of history. When a man reads all the important documents on a big subject, such as the birth, progress, and death of the British Empire in India, and then describes it in a series of orderly chapters, he is manifestly a historian. When a man lives through a series of important events, observing them with a clear, steady gaze, and sets down his impressions of them while they still have the freshness of immediacy, is he not writing historically? The organization is different, but it corresponds more closely to our actual experience of life; and although it is discontinuous, it is not haphazard. No historian is truly impersonal, however

*"On the Day of the Last Judgment, when men's souls are led to the Bar by great angels who, during the proceedings, will stand dozing like gendarmes with their chins resting on their white gloves folded on the pommels of their swords, and when God the Father with his long white beard, looking the way members of the Institute paint him in church cupolas, after questioning me about what I have done, questions me about everything to which I have lent the complicity of my eyes, he will doubtless ask me: 'Creature whom I made human and good, have you by any chance seen the bullfight at the Barrière du Combat, with five great famished bulldogs tearing to pieces some poor, thin old donkey incapable of defending itself?' To which I will reply: 'Alas, no, Lord, I have seen something worse than that: I have seen a *coup d'état.*' "

much he may pretend to be. The kind of history typified by the Goncourt *Journal* is more frankly personal than an organized historical study, that is all. It is not less valuable.

Other examples come to mind. William Hickey was a middle-class Englishman who wasted his youth in delightfully riotous living, had an unexpected but not unmerited success as a British official in the East, and in his old age wrote, largely for his own and his friends' diversion, a memoir of his life.* Rakish, sometimes vulgar in a jolly damn-your-eyes sort of way, sometimes immensely funny, it is a contribution to the history of British India, and a mirror of English manners in the time of George III.

Gaius Plinius Caecilius Secundus, called the younger Pliny, was a Roman financial and administrative expert who published, about A.D. 110, nine volumes of his letters to his friends. They are graceful little causeries on scores of different subjects: the great eruption of Vesuvius, the death of the epigrammatist Martial, problems of education, glimpses of popular religion, an important state trial. (He designed them, it would seem, to rival or to outdo Cicero's letters, which are on the whole far less polished and were usually not meant for publication.) Read as essays, they are quite charming, for Pliny was a cultivated man, naturally kind and sympathetic. But they are also a sort of autobiography, far more diverse and rather less egoistic than most personal memoirs. And further, since nearly all the conventional historians who described the reign of the emperor Trajan disappeared during the Dark Ages, Pliny's letters are a precious history of his own time.

Ranke said that the historian's job was to describe *wie es eigentlich gewesen*, "how it really happened"; but he did not explain what "it" was. And "it" can be either the majestic movement of diplomacy and war or the bewildering confusion of immediate experience. Read a few chapters in the *Cambridge Modern History*, and you will get a sober, balanced, instructive account of the reign of Charles II; but read Samuel Pepys his diary, and you will be far more likely to see how it really happened, how it looked, how it felt. Pepys saw the fire of London as it burned; he suffered through the plague; he watched the scandalous behavior of Charles and his paramours, and was disgusted. Better than any historian, he makes us see the blaze, share the terror, gag with the disgust. As the German scholar Aby Warburg used to say, "the dear God is found in details"; it is the brilliantly observed, vividly recorded details that make the essential merit of the Goncourt *Journal*.   GILBERT HIGHET

*A selection, edited by Peter Quennell, was published in the spring of 1962 by Dutton under the title of *The Prodigal Rake*.

CHANNELS

Two Cheers for Mediocrity

That time of year has come around again when we are faced with the beginning of a new television season. One discovers this by looking at the calendar: come September, oysters are in season and the New Year is observed at NBC, CBS, and ABC. It is the sort of thing one learns to accept on faith, like the vernal equinox, for there are really no outward and visible signs. The names of a few programs may change, but the programs themselves are immutable. Under the circumstances, it makes very little sense to embark upon a discussion of what we may expect from television this year. For the most part, we will get exactly what we got last year.

Still, there is no need to sulk. If we cannot ruminate upon what we will get, we can at least stop to consider what we would want. I have given this matter some thought, at odd moments from time to time, and inevitably I find myself recalling a program that I watched with some regularity over a period of three years. It was called *Hennesey*, and it employed the limited talents of Jackie Cooper, Roscoe Karns, and some other people whose names I never really knew.

It was, of course, a series. Drama on television must be cast as a series. From coast to coast there simply are not enough literate men and women to create new characters and new environments for some seventy-five to one hundred hours of television every week. Being a series, it had a general theme, which it pursued lazily from week to week. In the case of *Hennesey*, it was a very simple theme—*Hennesey* dealt with love. This in itself made *Hennesey* somewhat exceptional, for television rarely has any time for love in its series programs. It happens I am personally convinced that Matt Dillon sneaks into Miss Kitty's bedroom once in a while, but the program has never come right out and said so—it just smirks about it now and then. That and David Susskind's interminable love affair with David Susskind are about the only weekly romances I can think of.

Hennesey was not only about love—it was outspoken about it and it was reasonable about it. During the first year of the series, the hero and heoine became inter-

ested in each other; during the second year they fell in love; they were engaged during the last year, and in the final program they married. Along the way they were pleasantly sentimental about each other, and the program got along with a mere half-dozen misunderstandings, none of them serious. In short, it was a love affair that progressed in the fashion of most love affairs.

Each episode had a plot, but none of them was memorable. As evidence of this I adduce the fact that for the life of me I can't remember a single one. I do recall that some were amusing and some serious, and a few were good adult nonsense. I recall also that every now and then a plot so bad came along that I was tempted to rise, cross the living room, and turn the set off. But these were very few. Most of the time I was content to sit and watch.

The characters, of course, were caricatures. There never has been a young doctor quite as noble as Hennesey, or a sentimental, gruff old admiral quite as sentimental and gruff as his particular admiral, or a nurse quite as clever and true as whatever-her-name-was. But once again, you can't be subtle about the delineation of character for thirty minutes every week, and at least if these were caricatures, they were caricatures of real people. Ben Casey is a caricature of a caricature, and that gets a good deal too far out. It is possible to concede that people do exist who, if you suppressed all their characteristics but one, would resemble Hennesey. To that trifling extent the characters were true to life.

*N*ow, I have not made much of a case for *Hennesey*, and I feel obliged to defend my low-pressure affection for the program. I can express it in a few words: *Hennesey* was consistently mediocre. I could turn it on, any Monday evening, confident that it would be neither very good nor very bad. What is more, I could miss it any Monday evening when I had something better to do, because I knew very well that I really wasn't missing a thing.

Mediocrity, I suspect, is exactly what I want from television. I am quite certain that I don't want great art—at any rate, I don't want very much of it. Great art exacts a price from the viewer: he ceases to be a mere viewer and becomes a participant, working quite as hard as the artist worked. I enjoy that sort of thing as much as the next man, but I am not up to it every night of the week, and I find also that a living room is not the setting for so exacting an enterprise. Needless to say, the talent does not exist to keep stuffing the maw of television with great art, but if it did exist, and did take over television, I might get rid of my set and forget the whole thing.

What I want from television is something innocuous, done with reasonably good taste, which neither insults my intelligence nor makes demands upon it. I want to be able to watch television when I am so inclined, half-watch it when other things are drifting through my mind, and turn it off without a moment's regret when important affairs call me. In short, I want programs like *Hennesey* to be available when television beckons.

And of course it does beckon—it always has. After I have put in a long day burning with a hard, gemlike flame, or trying to, I find myself enticed by the notion of a quiet evening of sheer mediocrity, laving the body and soothing the soul, while all the busy neurons snap back into position and doze. I want the television set to do all the work, and I will be ever grateful to it, so long as it is careful not to insult me in the process.

It is for this reason that I welcome the flood of documentary programs that Mr. Minow appears to have forced upon television. They are almost invariably mediocre. They cannot often be very good because the amount of labor that must be put into a good documentary brings it beyond the means of television, which loses a potful of money on every one as it is. But they cannot often be very bad because they deal with real things and real persons, and that is almost always interesting. All in all, they are as soothing as *Hennesey*. That is to say, I can watch them with my shoes off. Imagine watching Eugene O'Neill with your shoes off! It simply wouldn't be fitting.

But we must also face the fact that television is as hard on mediocrity as it is on quality. *Hennesey* had a modestly good rating and stayed around for three years, but anyone with an ounce of showbiz know-how could have told you that it would never move the all-purpose detergent like a good earthy drama about this Jimmy Stewart-type fellow who is in some cute business like he sells meerschaum pipes and he has this Mickey Rooney-type eight-year-old son by his deceased first wife and he is being chased by this Loretta Young-type schoolteacher with the help of a lovable but eccentric housekeeper (who is really one of the family) and for a gimmick let's make the housekeeper a retired trapeze artist! So *Hennesey*, in fact, is no longer with us this season, and at this writing it also looks bad for the *Dick van Dyke Show*, and as for documentaries—let the FCC remove the pressure for four minutes and the documentaries will vanish from television between one issue of *TV Guide* and the next.

It won't make a great deal of difference. I shall simply go back to reading mediocre books, which are always in good supply. It isn't as relaxing as television, because you have to focus more sharply. But there are no commercials, and you are never disturbed by someone walking between you and the page. The more I think of the idea, the better I like it. Where is that new John O'Hara?
STEPHEN WHITE

COME OVER
AND SEE
FOR YOURSELF

"The lands . . . are all most beautiful. . . . The people all

go naked, men and women . . . they are artless and gen-

erous with what they have, to such a degree as no one

would believe but he who had seen it. . . ."

CHRISTOPHER COLUMBUS, 1493

In the centuries since Columbus, America has beckoned to the homeless and hungry of many lands, but not until recently to the foreign tourist. Loudly as we praise our rocks and rills, we have never seemed seriously to believe that anyone from anywhere else could wish to visit us of his own free will. Now all that is changing. With an initial $2,700,000 Congressional appropriation, the government has launched a massive "Visit U.S.A." program supported by come-hither posters in many lands abroad and by a new United States Travel Service to assist all comers hither and thither. There have been press conferences by Voit Gilmore, the Service's director. There have been embarrassing questions by foreign journalists—such as, where did you get the statistics circulated overseas that a foreigner could vacation in the United States for just $98 a week? Do you imagine Europeans eating only in drugstores and automats, and where in New York City do you expect them to pitch a tent?

While as anxious as Mr. Gilmore to attract visitors to America, and not bent on challenging his economics, HORIZON wishes only to forewarn foreign travelers against any false conceptions that might be engendered by the USTS's advertising. Friendly visitors from Britain (below) must expect to see home-grown celebrations of our revolt against the mother country. The voyager in the land of freedom must expect to find his movements limited in the interests of the general traffic flow (opposite); and the pilgrim to our national shrines, panoramas, and Western pleasances may find that somehow others got there before he did. Drawings by William Charmatz supplement the posters of the United States Travel Service on these pages, to remind any latter-day Columbus of what he should be prepared to discover.

TRAVEL A NEW WORLD
SEE THE U.S.A.

THE CAPITOL · WASHINGTON, D.C.

YORKTOWN

116

ENCODE ME, MY SWEET ENCODABLE YOU

By ⑈0 2 ⑉0 ⑈000 2⑈ 0 30 ⑈ ⑉ ⑈0 ⑉8 ⑉ ⑉ 5⑈

That's my name up there at the top of these columns, and I want to say right away what a thrill it is to see it in print. There's nothing like a by-line to give someone a sense of his own identity.

Actually that isn't the name I was born with. My legal name is William K. Zinsser. My family gave it to me, and I think that was very nice of them. But ⑈0 2 ⑉0 ⑈000 2⑈ 0 30 ⑈ ⑉ ⑈0 ⑉8 ⑉ ⑉ 5⑈ is my new name, given to me by the Chase Manhattan Bank just last year. The bank went to a lot of trouble to think it up and to make it different from anybody else's. Believe it or not, there isn't another ⑈0 2 ⑉0 ⑈000 2⑈ 0 30 ⑈ ⑉ ⑈0 ⑉8 ⑉ ⑉ 5⑈ in the whole world, and that's a mighty big thing to be able to say.

My new name isn't an easy one to catch at first. Sometimes I look at it on my checks, where the bank has so kindly imprinted it in magnetic ink, and I think "Is that really me?" and then I realize it really is. The bank assures me that it has a machine which can read my name "with incredible speed and accuracy."

What an assurance that is! I have a friend at Chase Manhattan who can read my name as easy as John Doe. The fact that my friend is a machine, that the personal element has gone out of banking, ought to bother me. But then I stop to think how much pleasure I give him.

See how his 200-watt eyes blink with joy as he runs his sensitized tongue over my magnetized checks and realizes that it is *me*, his old buddy. See the incredible speed and accuracy with which he taps out—for whatever human employees may be left at my branch—the two words that they need to know: ZINSSER and OVERDRAWN. See how the vice-presidents join hands and dance around the faithful computer, showering him with praise. It is such vignettes as this that make modern America a dynamic place to live in.

I'll confess that I resisted the shift to electronic banking at first. That was well over a year ago, when the bank sent me several hundred checks in a new format with my new name printed on them, and ordered me to start using them right away. I hated them thoroughly.

What annoyed me most, however, were the directives that accompanied them. These were awash in self-congratulation over the electronic feat. Now, boasted the bank, it would be able to serve me better, give me more efficient treatment, process my checks faster. But I had no complaint with the way the bank was serving me before. If anything, I want a bank that will process my checks slower and give me more time to cover them.

Banks may have many defects, but slowness is not one. An electronic computer will need to move with the speed of light to outrace an old-fashioned human banker in asking for interest due, or demanding extra collateral on a loan when the stock market drops. Obviously the bank had decided to install an electronic system for its *own* convenience but was trying to persuade me that it was really for *my* convenience.

Such tactics cried out for counterattack. I hurried to my bank and, by cleverly applying to different tellers, obtained enough of the old-fashioned checks to last a year. It was the happiest check-writing year of my life, made all the more pleasant by the testy notes that I kept receiving from the bank as the year wore on.

"Our records show," the notes said, "that you are not now using your encoded checks." (This at least proved that real people were still keeping records over there.) "If you have a supply of checks printed in magnetic ink but have not started using them, please commence using these checks and destroy all un-encoded checks you may have."

I couldn't commence using the new checks because I had thrown them away the day they arrived. I went on flooding the bank with old ones. I was a man possessed, or at least not un-enpossessed. There are not many pleasures left to the individual in this organized society, but one of them is to use un-encoded checks when the Chase Manhattan Bank is trying to encode you.

One day, of course, the old checks ran out and I had to surrender. Since then I've grown accustomed to my new name, possibly because it is turning up on other forms as well. Recently I received several hundred deposit slips with my encoded name on them.

"Please use these tickets for every deposit you make," said the accompanying note. "Your co-operation will insure accuracy in maintaining your account. . . . It's a good idea to keep a supply of deposit tickets handy wherever you might be—at home, at your office, in your car." It is nice to know the three places where the Chase Manhattan Bank thinks I am most likely to be. (It's also nice to know what the Chase Manhattan Bank thinks is "a good idea.") But there are several other places where I might just be instead, such as the ball park or the bar, especially if they keep hounding me. There are limits beyond which I will not be enpushed.

After all, I've got to preserve *some* individuality. Any month now the telephone company is going to take away my phone exchange—lovable old YU 8—and give me a seven-digit number that is all my own, unlike any other number in the country, which some machine will learn with incredible speed and accuracy, even if nobody else does, and that shift is *really* going to be hard to fight. The phone company is already taking ads telling us what a tremendous favor this will be to everyone who owns a phone. Honestly, the kindness of these big companies is enough to enmelt the heart.